Introducing Moral Issues

Joe Jenkins

Heinemann Educational Publishers,
Halley Court, Jordan Hill, Oxford OX2 8EJ
a division of Reed Educational & Professional Publishing Ltd

OXFORD PORTSMOUTH NH (USA) CHICAGO
MELBOURNE AUCKLAND IBADAN
GABORONE JOHANNESBURG BLANTYRE

© Joe Jenkins 1994

First published 1994

A catalogue record for this book is available from the British Library Cataloguing in Publication Data.

ISBN 0 435 30297 3

02 01
10 9

Designed and produced by Gecko Ltd, Bicester, Oxon

Illustrated by Chris Rothero and Harvey Collins

Printed and bound by Bath Press Ltd, Avon, England

Acknowledgements

The Publishers would like to thank the following for permission to reproduce photographs:
M. Abrahams/Network Photographers p.27 (right); Amnesty International p.93; K. Bernstein/Frank Spooner Pictures pp.4, 39 (right); Camera Press pp.39 (top), 63 (top); Format Partners pp.30, 35, 44, 76, 77; Greenpeace Communications p.95; Robert Harding Picture Library pp.46, 51, 87; Hutchison Library pp.8, 13; Impact Photos pp.20, 22 (bottom), 29, 64, 83; Joe Jenkins p.84; P. Lowe/Network Photographers pp.41, 43; Magnum Photos pp.27 (left), 49 (top); Network Photographers p.66; North News p.69 (right); Philip Parkhouse pp.69 (left), 72, 75; Picturepoint p.86; Chris Ridgers p.67; RSPCA p.85; Science Photo Library pp.10, 12, 17 (top), 17 (middle), 17 (bottom), 73, 80; Syndication International p.50; John Tramper p.63 (bottom); Philip Von Recklinghausen/Frank Spooner Pictures p.49 (bottom); Fiona Watson/Survival International p.89 (top); C. Wright/Format Partners p.53; Art Zamur/Frank Spooner Pictures p.22 (top); Zefa UK p.89 (bottom).

The Publishers would like to thank Impact Photos (solvent abuser, right) and Rex Features (Somali child, left) for permission to reproduce the cover photographs.

The Publishers would like to thank the following for permission to reproduce copyright material:
Age Concern England for the extracts from 'How will it feel to be old?' on p.54 and the two advertisements on p.55; Amnesty International, British Section, for the reproduction of their logo and text on p.93 (top); Amnesty International, International Secretariat, for the article 'The penalty for throwing stones' on p.93 (bottom); © *Buzz* magazine, the Citizenship Foundation, 63 Charterhouse Street, London, WC1M 6HJ, for the quiz 'How violent are you?' on p.56; *The Cartoonist* and Steven Appleby for the cartoon '3 Ways to Cheat Death' on p.19; *The Cartoonist* and John Hunt for the cartoon 'Lenny' on p.33; Christian Aid for their poem 'On the Streets' from *Streetwise* on p.65, the statement from *Why Christian Aid?* on pp.90–1 and the advertisement on p.91; © Crown Copyright for the use of text from the poster 'Drugs and solvents', reproduced with the permission of The Controller of Her Majesty's Stationery Office on p.82; Doctors for a Woman's Choice on Abortion (DWCA) for the extract taken from their leaflet 'Why we believe that the woman herself should make the abortion decision...' on p.77; Geraldine Doyle of The Children's Society for the article 'Leeds safe houses' featured in the Society magazine *Gateway* on p.65; © EMAP Images for the article 'Splat is back' on p.61; Kahlil Gibran for the quotations from *The Prophet* published by William Heinemann on pp. 18, 44; © *Guardian* for the extract 'A joyrider speaks' on p.69 and the article 'Deadly consequences' on p.69; Health Education Authority for the advertisements on pp.78, 79; C. M. Kay for the Reflections extracts from *Story of Stories*, with the kind permission of her daughter Dee Harkin on pp.6–7; Sheila Kitzinger for the quotations from *Being Born* on p.17; Maggy Ling for the cartoon 'Bet their lungs don't look so glamorous' on p.37; Mercury Express for the article 'My twin miracles' by Rachel Murphy on p.81; Joe Miller for the Earth poem on p.47; *New Internationalist* for the quotation 'Violence is sexist' on p.57; © *New York Times* for the extract 'The story of Sniffles' by Ann Roiphe on p.18; Oxfam for the extracts from the leaflet 'It's an unfair world' on p.90; Press Association for the article 'Too much TV violence' on p.57; *Shout* magazine, © D. C. Thompson, for the letters on p.32; Surgical Advisory Service for their advertisement on p.39; Tetra Films for the extracts from *The Morning After* on p.75; Terry Waite for use of his homecoming speech on p.92.

The Publishers have made every effort to trace copyright holders. However if any material has been incorrectly acknowledged, we would be pleased to correct this at the earliest opportunity.

The Publishers would like to thank W. Owen Cole for being religious studies consultant for this book.

The Author would like to thank the following for their support, guidance and inspiration in the writing of this book:
Tristan Boyer, Professor Suheil Bushrui, Center for International Development and Conflict Management at the University of Maryland (USA), Cheltenham and Gloucester College of Higher Education, Ben Jones, Patrick Ledeboer, Trish Ledeboer, Professor Matthew Lipman, Jack Mapanje, Aileen Milne, Jamie Roberts, Khalid Roy of Islamic Relief, Professor Ann-Margaret Sharp, Alison Sims, Diana Veasey, Sue Walton and Religious Studies teachers everywhere.

This book is dedicated to my daughters Laura and Louise.

CONTENTS ••••••••••••••••••••••••••••

1 INTRODUCTION ••••••••••••••••••••••••••

A changing world

We live in a world that always seems to be changing. Over the last century life for most people has changed enormously. Somebody who was fourteen in 1900 probably would not recognize the world as it is today. For instance, they would be amazed to learn that there are four hundred million (400 000 000) motor cars in the world, that we can send live pictures right across the world in a matter of seconds or that 35 000 people every day starve to death in our world. They would be amazed to find computer games, video cameras, microwave ovens, tiny portable televisions and CD players in many of our homes.

*T*HINGS TO DO

Imagine you are a fourteen year old born in 1886. You find a time capsule and travel into the modern world. List some of the things that you'd find very different and some things that might have remained unchanged.

Although human beings have been able to change many things in the world, an important question is, **do we as human beings really change**? Would a person who was a fourteen year old in 1900 really *feel* any differently from you? Here are some things that they might wonder about and some of the questions they might want to ask:

- *Why do people treat each other badly?*
- *What is right and what is wrong?*
- *What does the future hold?*
- *Will I get married and have children one day?*
- *How did everything get here?*
- *What is a friend?*
- *Will I be happy in my life?*
- *What will make me unhappy?*
- *Can I make myself happy?*
- *Why do people argue?*
- *How should we treat animals?*

*I*N GROUPS

These are just some questions that they might ask. In groups of three or four list some of the questions you'd like to ask. Discuss some of these questions.

What matters?

Human beings have always asked these questions. If we went back 100, 500, 1000 or 2000 years, we should find people asking these same questions. If we could travel into the future, to the year 2100, we would probably find people still asking 'What matters?'

It is part of human nature to ask questions. Because we can think about the past, and can imagine the future, we often ask questions about life and death. Perhaps one of the most important questions of all is, 'What matters?'.

Every day in our world, 35 000 people die from starvation

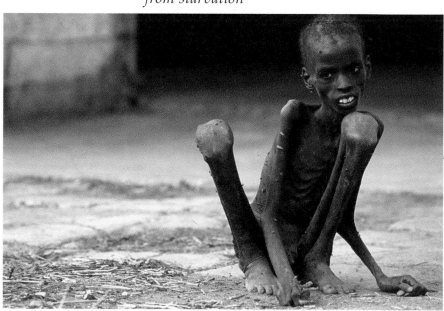

The question can be answered in many different ways.

1 You are a thirteen year old living in a country suffering from war and famine. Every day is a struggle to survive. How might you answer the question 'What matters?'

2 You live in a comfortable house with a happy family. You are thirteen and in the second year of a large comprehensive school. What matters?

3 You live with your mum in a large block of flats in a city. You haven't got much money but have enough to eat and you've got a roof over your head. What matters?

4 You are a famous pop star. You've got all the possessions you want. What matters?

5 You are living in a hut high up in the mountains. You are surrounded by beautiful scenery, lovely animals and you grow your own food. What matters?

We find that people, wherever they live or however they live, will probably answer the question 'What matters?' in the same way. Some of these answers may include:

● *My happiness matters.*
● *The happiness of my loved ones matters.*
● *My health matters.*
● *How I get on with other people matters.*

Sometimes, the question 'What matters?' may make people ask more questions. They may say that these are the questions that really matter:

● *What happens to me when I die?*
● *Why was I born?*
● *Why does everything have to die?*
● *How should we behave towards other living things?*
● *Why should we treat other living things in a certain way?*

World religions

Since the earliest of times people have asked these questions. They are not easy to answer. However, millions of people believe that we have been given help and guidance in answering them, and the answers are to be found in the world religions that have been given to human beings.

Although we can send machines into space, send satellite pictures across the world and travel across the world in a matter of hours, we still have to face the important question 'What matters?'. Whoever we are, however and wherever we live, we are all basically the same and have to face these same questions.

In this book you will be introduced to some of these questions, and to some of the answers that have been given about what matters. You will be looking at what problems face you as individuals, as members of our society and as human beings on planet Earth. You will be asked to think about these matters – matters of life and death.

Some of the possible answers will come from the world religions which have guided human beings for hundreds of years and continue to guide them today. Many of the answers will be taken from the Bible, made up of the Old and New Testaments, that has had a great influence on our own particular society. Other answers will be taken from the sacred scriptures of the Bahá'í, Buddhist, Hindu, Jewish, Muslim and Sikh religions. These books are very important to millions of people across the world today.

The ideas contained in them may help you to find some answers in your own life and, in doing so, help you in your search for happiness and understanding.

2 IDEAS ABOUT GOD ••••••••••••••••••

You may know people who have different ideas about God. There are some people who do not believe there is a God at all. They are called **atheists**. Other people think that what is called God is too great for people to know and understand. They are called **agnostics**.

However, all through the ages people have feared the great forces of Nature and also felt the wonder of the world around them. So they have worshipped what they call 'God' in many different ways.

All over the world God is called by different names in the different languages and religions that fill our planet. God is described as 'Great', 'Goodness', 'Life', 'Truth', 'Beauty', 'Love' – in fact the highest and best words that people can think of.

There are many different books about God. These books are called **sacred scriptures**. Some people think that their idea of God or their book about God is the only true one, and so people sometimes do not understand each other and are afraid of each other.

These fears and misunderstandings have sometimes led to wars. People have actually killed other human beings whose idea of God seems different from their own. This is very sad, because all the sacred scriptures teach that killing is wrong.

These scriptures also contain stories that tell of great teachers, wise men and women in all ages, who have taught people to treat each other with respect and love. Some of these stories are very old and have been passed on to us, telling us things about matters of life and death.

To begin to understand the different people that live in our world we need to understand something about their religions. Although this book does not have the space to go into detail about the world religions, when it can, it will tell you what religious people feel about matters of life and death.

As an introduction to some of these religions here are some reflections.

Reflections

'My name is Radha. I come from India. India is a very large country where there are many people and many religions. I am a Hindu and my friend Ajit Singh is a Sikh. There are also Buddhists, Christians, Muslims and Bahá'ís in India. What you call God, Hindus call Brahman. Brahman is the One hidden in all beings everywhere. The real self in all beings.'

'I am Ajit Singh, a Sikh, which means a disciple or a follower. We are followers of Sat Nam, the Timeless Truth.'

'My name is Ananda. I come from Sri Lanka. We Buddhists do not give a name to that which we think is beyond names. The word "Buddha" means "the Enlightened One", the wise and knowing One, the One who found out that it was our own ideas about ourselves and our selfishness, which cause misery and suffering in all sorts of ways. We are ignorant when we are selfish, and so we learn through many lives that one must be unselfish to find real peace. Knowing this peace is called "Nirvana".

'I am a Native American Indian called Lacota. We are many tribes but we all worship the Great Spirit which is everywhere. Because the Great Spirit is to be found in all things, we treat the planet, its animals and people with respect.'

'I am Jewish. My name is Samuel. We believe that God's name Yhwh is too holy to be used often, so we call Him Adonai (Lord). The name Yhwh means Eternal – that which will be for ever and for ever. Our Bible tells the history of our people and contains the laws that God gave us. We call the first five books

of this Bible the Torah. They were revealed to Moses – our Great Leader and Teacher – long ago. The laws in the Torah help us and guide us in our lives today.'

'My name is Tom. I am a Christian. We believe in the One Eternal God and we believe He sent His son Jesus Christ to show His Holy Spirit in humankind. Jesus taught that God who created the earth and the universe is like a loving Father and we are all His children. We believe that we must try to treat each other with respect and love, because the Kingdom of God is within each one of us. God is Love.'

'I am a Muslim and my name is Hassan. We believe that there is no God but Allah and Muhammad is His Prophet. There have been several prophets (or great human beings) in history who have told people about the One God Allah, to whom we must all submit. The East and the West are God's – therefore whichever way we turn, there is God. Truly God is immense, all-knowing, all-loving, kind and merciful.'

'My name is Richard. I am a Bahá'í. Bahá'u'lláh, the Founder of our Faith, teaches that there is only One God, although people call Him by different names. God is so very great we can never know Him unless He shows Himself to us in a way in which we can understand. That is why, from time to time, He chooses One pure enough to be like a polished mirror to reflect His Light. These are the Founders of the religions. Through them we become nearer to God. The name of our Founder, Bahá'u'lláh, means "The Glory of God".'

'I am African. My name is Awo. Africa is a huge country and has many religions. Because our country is so large our languages are different in different parts of Africa, therefore we have different names for the Great One. He is everywhere and is Good. We do not see Him as a person with our eyes, but we know Him in our heart.'

FOR YOUR FOLDERS

1 What do the following words and phrases mean: atheist, agnostic, sacred scriptures?

2 Why do you think people have killed each other in the name of religion?

3 Why are the sacred scriptures so important to followers of the world religions?

4 List some of the things the world religions have in common.

5 Explain what you think the following phrases mean:
● 'One light, many lanterns'
● 'God is One'.

6 Why do you think it has been said that there will be no peace in the world without peace between the world religions?

7 Design a poster using the symbols of the world religions, on the theme 'Many voices, one God'.

CLASS DEBATE

In a recent survey in Britain, 70% of people interviewed said they believed in a God. Although many of the people do not go to church or other places of worship, they believe that the world was created and has **meaning**. Organize a class debate on the motion 'This House believes that God exists'.

3 *SEEING IS BELIEVING* ••••••••••••••••••

What people believe in affects the way they think, feel and act. For instance, if you believe that your chair is just about to break you probably won't sit in it. If you believe that a certain place is dangerous, you'll probably stay away from there. If you believe that people should be treated kindly, you won't bully anyone.

Also, believing that certain ideas make sense and other ideas are nonsense will guide your thinking. If you believe that an idea is sensible and that it is a good idea, you will be more likely to rely on it, and it may affect the way you look at life.

For thousands of years people have **believed** that the world is created, has a purpose and is the work of a Higher Mind. These **beliefs** have affected the way they have treated the world and its peoples.

Beliefs are very powerful things. Africans, Aborigines, Bahá'ís, Buddhists, Christians, Hindus, Amazonian Indians, Native American Indians, Jews, Muslims, Sikhs and others believe that the world has meaning. They believe that the world was **created**. They believe that all human beings have within them 'a divine spark'. They believe that when our bodies die, our lives will continue. They believe that this life is not the end of existence but a time and place in which we learn a great many things.

If you believe that life really has no meaning, there is no God and we're here just to be as comfortable as we can be, then you could be called a **materialist**.

Many Christians believe that the sick can be cured at Lourdes, in France

FOR DISCUSSION

Here are some ideas about beliefs.

- *'Beliefs are like rules for what we do, say or think.'*
- *'Beliefs are strong ideas.'*
- *'Beliefs are ideas that tell us what we know.'*
- *'Beliefs affect the way people behave.'*

TASKS

- *Can you know something without believing it?*
- *Can you believe something without knowing it?*
- *Can you believe something you doubt?*
- *Can you doubt something you believe?*
- *Can you understand something without believing it?*
- *Can you believe something without understanding it?*

KEY QUESTION

If you believe that the world has no meaning, the universe has no meaning, and life has no meaning, do you think that this might affect the way you see life, feel about life, and speak and act in life?

KEY IDEA

Everybody believes in something. Our beliefs affect the way we think about life, and the way we behave towards others.

IN GROUPS

In groups of three or four, discuss the following. Afterwards, report back to the whole class.

● Belief is like trust. I believe that when I wake up tomorrow everything will be the same as it is today. How would it affect your life if everything had changed?

● Is it hard for somebody to believe in a God when a member of their family has just died?

Powerful beliefs

● Hitler *believed* he was doing good. Yet because of his beliefs six million Jewish people died in the Nazi concentration camps. Are beliefs sometimes dangerous?

● Millions of people pick up a newspaper and read their horoscopes every day. What do they *believe* in?

● If I fall in love I *believe* that in some way the person I've fallen in love with is 'special' or different from other people.

● Every year thousands of Christians, who

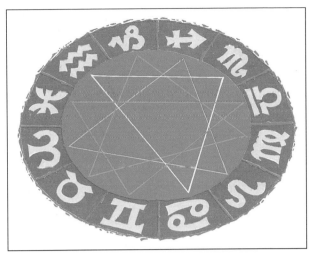

It's in the stars ... millions of people believe that horoscopes can tell us things about ourselves

are ill and in great pain, travel to Lourdes in France. They *believe* that if they pray at the shrine of the Virgin Mary, they will be cured, or will be able to accept their suffering.

● Many people have claimed they have cured themselves of diseases like cancer. They have visualized (seen themselves) getting well and told themselves they will be well. They have *believed* that the workings of the mind are stronger than matter. This is called **mind over matter.**

● People 'believe' in science or maths, but they may not really understand them. Can you think of a belief that is all your own that hasn't come from other people?

● A **placebo** is a *make-believe* medicine. It is unable to do anything. A patient takes it believing it will make them better, and it often does.

THINKING POINT

'We are what we think.'
(Dhammapada, Buddhist Scripture)

4 MEANINGS OF LIFE ●●●●●●●●●●●●●●

Have you ever thought about how amazing life is? Our planet lies in the galaxy called the **Milky Way**. There are thought to be 100 billion galaxies each containing some 10 billion trillion (10 000 000 000 000 000 000 000) stars and planets.

We don't know if other forms of life exist on these other planets, but we do know that our planet, which orbits round the sun is in just the right position for life to develop. If it were any closer to the sun it would be too hot for life as we know it. If it were any further from the sun it would be too cold for life to develop. The Earth and all the other planets which orbit round our sun, together with the sun itself, are called the **solar system**.

The Earth from space

In different parts of the world and at different times, different religions have developed. All of these religions have provided men and women throughout the ages with answers to these questions. Even though they have developed in different places, and even though they may have never known about each other, they have answered these questions in similar ways.

Question 1
Is the world just an accident or was it made?

An answer from the Ancient Egyptians:
'The Lord of All, after having come into being says, "I am he who came into being ... when I came into being, the beings came into being, all the things came into being after I became."'

(The Book of Overthrowing Apophis)

An answer from Judaism:
'In the beginning, when God created the universe, the Earth was wild and barren. The raging ocean was covered in total darkness, and the power of God was moving over the water. Then God commanded, "Let there be light" – and light appeared.' (Genesis 1: 1–3)

An answer from the Native American Indians:
'At the beginning all things were in the mind of Wakonda (the Great Spirit), the Maker of all things.'

From these ancient teachings we can see that the world did not come into being by pure chance. It was created by a Supreme Being (the Lord of All, God, Wakonda).

Question 2
How does the way people look at life affect the way they treat others?

An answer from Christianity:
'Do not judge others, so that God will not judge you, for God will judge you in the same way as you judge others, and he will apply to you the same rules you apply to others.'

(Matthew 7: 1–2)

An answer from Hinduism:
'True religion is to love God, as God has loved them, all things, whether great or small.'

(Hitopadesa)

An answer from Islam:
'Do you love your Creator? Then love your fellow human beings.' (Hadith, 208)

An answer from Sikhism:
'A place in God's court can be attained only if we do service to others in the world.'

(Guru Granth Sahib, 26)

From the above teachings we can see that people who believe in a God and in a created universe feel that part of God's purpose is that human beings treat each other properly. However, some people who do not believe in a God, for instance Humanists, also believe that humans should treat each other properly.

'Humanists say that morality is about doing good and feeling good. It is about doing what is right and feeling right about it. Humanists do not look to a God for guidance on these matters, nor to a God-given code of behaviour.'

(Humanist Dipper)

THINGS TO DO
After reading this section design a poster on the theme 'A created world'.

FOR YOUR FOLDERS
1 According to the Ancient Egyptians, Judaism and the Native American Indians, is the world just an accident?

2 Explain in your own words what you think the Christian, Hindu, Muslim and Sikh religions mean by their answers to Question 2.

3 How do you think a person's beliefs might affect the way they treat other people? Use some of the above quotes in your answers.

4 Write down three beliefs you have (e.g. I believe that animals have rights). Explain briefly how these beliefs might affect the way you look at the world and behave in it.

5 THE MYSTERIES OF LIFE ••••••••••••

Mystery 1

Human beings are remarkable creatures. We have sent men to the moon, we can send live pictures by satellite across the planet, we can explore the atom with powerful instruments, and we can transplant a human heart. We have achieved many brilliant things. However, we can also destroy things and people. Human beings create wars, poverty, pollution, and cause dreadful suffering to their fellow beings, to animals and to the planet.

Here, then, is one mystery. How and why do human beings create such brilliant things yet also destroy so much?

Mystery 2

There are about 100 billion galaxies, each with an average of 10 billion trillion stars. Carl Sagan, a famous scientist says, 'To me it seems likely that the universe is brimming over with life. But to us humans, this is a mystery.' If we think about the huge universe we have to accept that we know very little about it. What do you think?

Mystery 3

Our planet is situated in just the right position in our solar system for life to survive. If our planet moved from its present orbit around the sun, everything would die. Do you think our planet got here by accident or was its position in the solar system planned? Why is our planet in its present position? How did it get here?

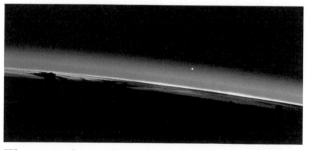

The ozone layer. Our planet is situated in just the right position in the solar system for life to survive. Is this coincidence or part of a plan?

Mystery 4

Some people who have 'medically died', and have been brought back to life by doctors, claim that when they died they 'left their bodies'. They went to a place full of light and even met other people they knew who had died before them. Many of these people believe that when our bodies die something continues to live. The mystery of life after death has puzzled people throughout the ages. Do you think there is life after death?

Mystery 5

Some religions teach that this is not our first life, nor will it be our last. They teach that after the death of the physical body our spirit or soul moves into another body. Our next life depends on how we've lived in this one.

'I have been born in every single place throughout the entire extension of space. Each and every physical form in existence, even the most ugly and miserable of all, seen or not seen by me, I have taken countless times.'

(Lama Zopa Rinpoche, a Tibetan Buddhist teacher)

This is called **reincarnation**. What do you think about it?

Mystery 6

Every day millions of people read their **horoscopes** in the papers. Although these horoscopes are very simple and often inaccurate, the science of astrology is very ancient and complicated. Do the great planets of our solar system affect the way we are? Do they influence us? What do you think?

Mystery 7

There are many ancient sites around the world that we know very little about. For instance, 3500 years ago the people of Britain brought 80 blocks of bluestone from the mountains of Wales. They were carried in a raft around the Welsh coast and into the River Avon. Then they were transported up rivers, through forests, and over moorlands and hills. They were finally pulled by rollers to Stonehenge where they were erected in two circles. The bluestones were later removed and replaced by the gigantic stones that still dominate the site today. Some of these stones weigh 26 tonnes. A professor of astronomy (the scientific study of the sun, moon, stars and other heavenly bodies), called Gerald Hawkins, says that these stones were used as an observatory and a computer. How could people so long ago make such a complicated computer and observatory? Why did they build Stonehenge?

In all these examples (there are many more) two questions keep coming up. These questions are 'How?' and 'Why?'. The way you answer these questions depends on how you see the world.

Stonehenge by moonlight

A spiritual viewpoint

Many people believe that as well as the world we can see (the physical, external world), there is also a hidden internal world – a spiritual world. They believe that:

- *There is a power bigger than themselves.*
- *There is something more to life than the physical world.*
- *There is a purpose to our lives.*
- *Our lives have a meaning.*
- *Everything we do in this life is very important, as it affects not only other people, but also the journey of our own soul or spirit.*
- *Death is not the end of our journey, but the beginning of a new adventure.*

FOR DISCUSSION

- *Why do human beings build such brilliant things yet destroy so much?*
- *How will we ever know if there is other life in the universe?*
- *How did our planet get here? Why do you think it got here?*
- *How might the great planets of our solar system affect our personalities and our lives?*
- *Do you think life is just one stopping off point on a great journey?*
- *Why do you think the ancient peoples of the world built observatories and computers?*
- *Why do some people believe that how we live in this life is very important?*

THINKING POINTS

'*There are many rooms in my Father's house.*'

(Jesus, in John 14: 2)

'*The more we find out, the more there is still to discover.*'

(Sikh teaching, Guru Granth Sahib, 5)

6 WHO AM I? •••••••••••••••••••••••

We all know certain things about ourselves. We know where we were born, the names of our parents, our likes and dislikes, the way we behave with friends, the things we own, the things we're good at.

Sometimes, people who know us well see things in us that we don't even see ourselves. As we grow up we begin to acquire **habits**. A habit is something we do – often without even thinking about it.

Key Questions 1

- *What habits have I acquired in my life?*
- *Are there some habits I sometimes forget I have?*

In our lives we have to try to get on with many different types of people. Like an actor we have to play different roles. If we are with one person we may act and speak very differently than if we are with another person. Look at Figure 1.

Key Questions 2

- *Am I a different person when I'm with different people?*
- *Do I sometimes forget who the real 'me' is?*

The mask you wear with a strict teacher might be very different from the one you wear when you're with a close friend. This can sometimes make you feel that you are more than one person. Some of these masks are more comfortable to wear than others. The mask you wear when you have to talk to a strict teacher may be very uncomfortable. The mask you wear when you're relaxing with a close friend might be very comfortable. In fact it might be so comfortable that you don't even notice it when you slip it on.

We learn quite quickly in life that we often have to put on masks. For instance, if we behaved with a strict teacher in exactly the same way as we behaved with our best friend, we might get into a bit of trouble.

Where do we learn these things? As we grow up we are influenced by many different people. When we're very young we usually learn things from our parents and perhaps our brothers and our sisters. We learn many things by **imitation** – by copying what we see from those around us.

Key Questions 3

- *Which people have influenced me?*
- *Who have I imitated and who do I imitate today?*
- *Are there some things that just come from 'me'?*

The number of influences increases as we get older. Look at Figure 2, which illustrates the many people who influence us.

Figure 1   I am a ...

grandparents

friends acquaintances

television

my country its culture, laws and religion

magazines

religion

newspapers

my school

teachers

advertising

books

parent(s)

close friends

my local community

pop music

family

Figure 2   Who influences me?

Sometimes, these influences can make us feel uncomfortable, discontented and even unhappy. For instance, I might wish that I looked like somebody in a magazine or on television. This can make life difficult at times. We may want to be somebody we're not.

KEY QUESTIONS 4

- *Why do we sometimes want to be somebody else?*
- *Why can't we just accept who we are and be happy with ourselves?*

When we were small children we never used to think about these things. But as we grow up we begin to change:

- *physically ... our bodies change*
- *mentally ... the way we think*
- *emotionally ... the way we feel.*

To help us develop into happy human beings we need good influences. We need people whom we can trust, whom we know are trying to help us in life, who are trying to

do their best for us. This idea of trust is a very important one.

KEY QUESTIONS 5

- *Whom do I trust?*
- *Why do I trust this person?*
- *How can I accept myself for what I am when so many people seem to want me to be different?*

Life is like a journey. We have seen that we develop and change physically, emotionally and mentally. If we are to be happy and contented in life, perhaps one of the first things we should do is ask the question, 'Who am I?'. We should try to accept ourselves as we are, and not always want to be like somebody else.

It's not always easy to be content and happy with ourselves. If we feel content and happy with the way we are getting on with others and feel happy with ourself, this could be called **self-esteem**.

The world religions all teach that every individual person is unique and special, and everybody's individuality should be respected. They teach that a human life comes from God and that this world is a place where we learn a great many things about ourselves.

'The Kingdom of God is within you.'

(Jesus, in Luke 17: 21)

'Ishvara (the Lord) dwells in the hearts of all creatures ....'

(Bhagavad-Gita 18: 61)

'So God created human beings, making them to be like Himself.'

(Genesis 1: 27)

IN GROUPS

In groups of about ten, discuss all the Key questions.

7 THE MIRACLE OF LIFE ● ● ● ● ● ● ● ● ● ● ● ●

In this section you will be encouraged to think about the amazing fact of life.

The photographs in this section show the development of life in a mother's womb. For people who believe there is more to life than we can see, life is a gift. It is precious. Every life has meaning.

THINKING POINTS

'If there were no man .... This world would be like a body without a soul.'
(Bahá'í teaching by 'Abdu'l-Bahá, Some Answered Questions, 188)

'Wasting this very precious human rebirth is many millions of times worse than losing universes full of precious jewels.'
(Lama Zopa Rinpoche, a Buddhist Teacher)

'Those who are born will surely die and the dead will be born again.'
(Hindu teaching, Bhagavad-Gita 2: 27)

'Allah fixes the time span for all things. It is He who causes both laughter and grief; it is He who causes people to die and to be born; it is He who causes male and female; it is He who will recreate us anew.'
(Muslim teaching, Qur'an 53: 42–7)

'The world and all that is in it belong to the Lord.'
(Jewish teaching, Psalms 24: 1)

'The dawn of a new day is the herald of a sunset. Earth is not your permanent home.'
(Sikh teaching, Guru Granth Sahib, 793)

Who are we?

All the world religions teach that human life has meaning. In the Bible the question is asked, 'Who are we?'. In the *Book of Psalms* the question is answered.

'When I look at the sky, which you have made, at the moon and the stars, which you set in their places – what is man, that you think of him: mere man, that you care for him? Yet you made him inferior only to yourself; you crowned him with glory and honour.'
(Psalms 8: 3–5)

Other answers to the question 'Who are we?' include the following ideas: God made all things; God cares for human beings; human life is very special, only God is greater than a human life; humans are wonderful beings. Because of these sorts of ideas Christians believe that the purpose of our life on earth is to:

'Love the Lord your God with all your heart, with all your soul, and with all your mind .... Love your neighbour as yourself.'
(Jesus, in Matthew 22: 37–9)

FOR DISCUSSION
● Life is very precious.
● Earth is not your permanent home.
● The purpose of life is to love others.

FOR YOUR FOLDERS

There are many ideas here about the miracle of life. Using some of the thinking points, design a poster on either 'The miracle of life' or 'The purpose of life'.

PHOTO SCAN

Look at the three photographs opposite, which show the development of a human being in the womb. Using some of the ideas in the captions, write a poem about what the photographs mean to you.

When you had been six months inside your mother's body you could hear her voice. Often when she spoke you moved, almost as if you could talk to her with your whole body. She spoke and you listened. Then you moved. She spoke again and you stayed still. Then, when she had finished speaking, you would move again. Loud bangs made you jump. ▼ **3**

1 *At the very beginning there was no you. Like a seed in a soft, round pod, a tiny egg lay deep inside your mother's body in her ovary. The egg was as small as this full stop.*

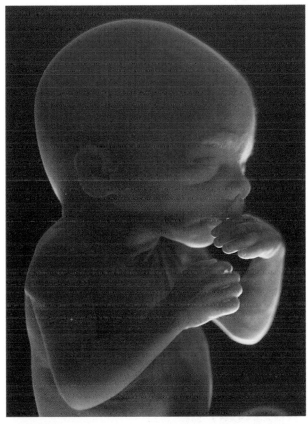

Nine or ten weeks after ▶ **2** *you had started to grow you could open and close your mouth. After twelve weeks you could make funny faces. You could frown, and press your lips together, and push your lips forward. Yet you still weighed only as much as a hen's egg in its shell.*

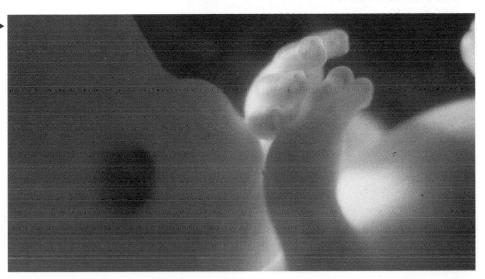

8 THE SECRET OF DEATH ••••••••••••

You would know the secret of death.
But how shall you find it unless
you seek it in the heart of life?
... For life and death are one, even
as the river and the sea are one.'

(Kahlil Gibran, The Prophet)

Death is often a bogey-word. People don't like talking about it. However, death is a fact of life. As the American comedian Woody Allen said, 'Nobody gets out of life alive.' Everything and everybody dies.

Because religions are concerned about the meaning of life, they have a lot to say about this one thing that nobody can escape, namely – death.

Despite the fact that death is part of life, it still makes us sad. We know that everything dies. This knowledge is not always easy to carry around.

The story of Sniffles

Read this newspaper article. It is about a Peruvian guinea-pig called Sniffles. At first, two guinea-pigs which the writer bought for her children strike her as being without thought or feeling. Then the female dies. Before long the male is lying around silently, with no interest in food. They assume he is sick, and that he, too, will die.

THE STORY OF SNIFFLES

Suddenly, frantically, Sniffles ran from one of the cages to the other, facing away from us, flipping over and over as if possessed of a demon, his eyes rolling in his head. Never before had he done this. He's dying, we thought. In the morning he was still there, his back to us. No turning of the head when we approached. He seemed to be getting smaller and his fur appeared as if it might at any moment slip off his tiny frame. He was looking at nothing. "Is he thinking about dying?" I asked one of the children. "Of course not," said one of our older daughters. "Man is the only animal who can imagine his own death." Suddenly, he turned around .... "He's going to live," said the children. He faced the room. He watched us again. ➤

With a certain horror I realised he had never been sick at all. Clearly, after initially not grasping the situation, he then had felt alone. He was grieving for his mate. He was almost driven mad with loneliness and grief. He had mourned and then, pushed by the force of life, he had returned, adjusted, joined us again. In some way in that small cage a creature had sensed death, had imagined it so well that loneliness nearly drove him to his own death, and then he had settled for mere existence, and accepted loss.'

*I*N PAIRS

Discuss the following.

● *What happened to Sniffles in this story?*
● *'He watched us again. With a certain horror I realised he had never been sick at all.'*

*C*LASS DISCUSSION

Some people have medically died, and felt themselves leaving their bodies – and then being brought back to their bodies. Read the author's interview below. What do you think about this?

A near-death experience

'I was painting the house. Suddenly the ladder slipped and I plunged to the floor. The next thing, I was floating up towards a bright, brilliantly bright room. It was a beautiful warm feeling. I walked into the room. Then I saw my father, who'd died three years before. I went to hug him. He put his hand up and smiled. He seemed to be saying to me, "Don't come near – you've got to go back. There are many things in your life that you have to do, and many things yet to learn." Just then I felt myself floating again. I was hovering above my body which was lying on a hospital bed surrounded by doctors and nurses. With a jolt, I felt myself return to my body.'

(Author's interview)

The ritual of burial

A **ritual** is a ceremony used at certain important occasions, such as birth, marriage and death. Why do people have rituals? It seems that rituals help people to feel connected with the past and to celebrate important times in their lives. Rituals also help people to find meaning in their lives.

> ### KEY QUESTION
> ● *Do you think rituals give meaning to life?*

The old man

'When my dad died I felt as if I'd lost something physical – I really felt I'd lost a leg. I was stumbling around. It was as if I'd been physically hit. When the funeral came along and I saw his coffin disappear into the furnace, and we sang, "Yea though I walk in the valley of death I will fear no ill", I began to cry.

'After the service my brother and I gathered up the "Old Man's" ashes, and walked up the hill by our house. It was winter and the snow touched the giant peaks of the distant mountains. A bitter wind whistled through our grief. We released his ashes, from the little urn.' (Author's interview)

The secret truth

The Christian belief in a life beyond death is described by St Paul:

'Listen to this secret truth. We shall not all die. But when the last trumpet sounds, we shall all be changed in an instant, as quickly as the blinking of an eye. For when the trumpet sounds, the dead will be raised, never to die again, and we shall all be changed into what is immortal; what will die must be changed into what cannot die. So when this takes place, and the mortal has been changed into the immortal, then the scripture will come true: "Death is destroyed: victory is complete. Where, Death, is your victory? Where, Death, is your power to hurt?"' (1 Corinthians 15: 51–58)

In Hindu scripture it is written:
'As one lays away a worn-out robe and takes a new one, so the Spirit puts by its garment of flesh and passes to inherit a new one.'
(Bhagavad-Gita, 2)

> ### CARTOON SCAN
> Often people like to make jokes about death.
>
> ● *What do you think the cartoon below is trying to say?*
> ● *Why do you think people sometimes make jokes about death?*

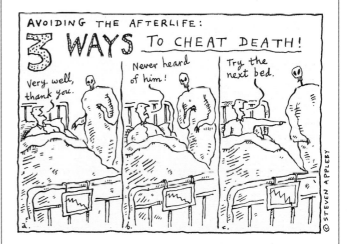

> ### TALKING POINT
> *'Let us try to live, so that when we come to die, even the undertaker will be sorry.'*
> (Mark Twain, American writer, author of Tom Sawyer and Huckleberry Finn)

> ### THINKING POINT
> *'Those who are born will surely die, and the dead will be born again ....'*
> (Hindu teaching, Bhagavad-Gita 2: 27)

9 INNER MEANINGS ••••••••••••••••••••••

All the world religions have holy books called sacred scriptures. These scriptures, it is believed, are **divinely inspired** – this means that they are given to human beings from a Higher Level. They contain guidelines about how people should live, and ideas about the meaning of life. Some of the scriptures are extremely old – for instance, the Hindu sacred scriptures known as the **Vedas** are at least 3500 years old.

The Gospels

In the New Testament of the Christian Bible there are books called the **Gospels**. These are writings concerned with the life and teachings of Jesus. In the Gospels many of Jesus' sayings are contained in **parables**. Parables are simple stories that have deep meaning. They can be read literally, just as stories, or as a way of finding greater meaning and understanding about life.

One of the most famous parables is the **Parable of the Good Samaritan,** in *Luke* 10: 25–37.

A teacher of the Law came up and tried to trap Jesus. 'Teacher,' he asked, 'what must I do to receive eternal life?'

Jesus answered him, 'What do the Scriptures say? How do you interpret them?'

The man answered, 'Love the Lord your God with all your heart, with all your soul, with all your strength, and with all your mind,' and 'Love your neighbour as you love yourself.'

'You are right,' Jesus replied, 'do this and you will live.'

It is the way people are like inside that is important, and not what they look like or where they come from

But the teacher of the Law wanted to justify himself, so he asked Jesus, 'Who is my neighbour?'

Jesus answered, 'There was once a man who was going down from Jerusalem to Jericho when robbers attacked him, stripped him, and beat him up, leaving him half dead. It so happened that a priest was going down the road; but when he saw the man, he walked on by, on the other side. In the same way a Levite also came along, went over and looked at the man, and then walked on by, on the other side. But a Samaritan who was travelling that way came upon the man, and, when he saw him, his heart was filled with pity. He went over to him, poured oil and wine on his wounds and bandaged them; then he put the man on his own animal and took him to an inn, where he took care of him. The next day he took out two silver coins and gave them to the innkeeper. "Take care of him," he told the innkeeper, "and when I come back this way, I will pay you whatever else you spend on him."'

And Jesus concluded, 'In your opinion, which one of these three acted like a neighbour towards the man attacked by the robbers?'

The teacher of the Law answered, 'The one who was kind to him.'

Jesus replied, 'You go, then, and do the same.'

Like all parables, the parable of the Good Samaritan can be understood at different levels. It can tell us many different things. Here are some of them:

Level 1 It is a story about a Samaritan helping a victim of a mugging.

Level 2 It is a story about a person who, during Jesus' time, many people hated just because they came from another country. Samaritans were thought of as being second-class citizens. This story is unexpected – it surprises the reader because nobody would expect a Samaritan to help a victim of mugging.

Level 3 In Jesus' time, the Jewish priests and Levites were regarded as being 'good people'. The parable shows that although people may appear good on the outside, they may in fact be evil inside. It's a story about the 'outer' and the 'inner' person.

Level 4 The Samaritan is good. He may be thought of as being an 'outsider' by society, but inwardly he is a good person.

Level 5 It is good to care for others and to help those in trouble.

Level 6 The Samaritan acts without expecting any reward.

*F*OR YOUR FOLDERS

1 Are there people in our society whom we regard as 'outsiders'?

2 Do we often judge people by external (outward) things, e.g. the country they come from, the clothes they wear?

3 Why do you think it is important that we 'look below the surface' of things?

4 Can you think of examples when you have helped somebody and not expected a reward?

5 Who do you think are the people in our world who need caring for?

6 What can be done by (a) governments; (b) pressure groups (groups that put pressure on governments to change situations, e.g. Greenpeace, Friends of the Earth, Oxfam, Amnesty International, Save the Children Fund); (c) individuals like yourselves, to change things for the better, as the Samaritan did for the victim of the mugging in the parable of the Good Samaritan?

10 TEACHINGS IN THE BIBLE • • • • • • • • •

The Ten Commandments

Nearly 3300 years ago the Jewish people received a set of laws and guidelines about how people should live. They were set down in their holy book known as the Torah. There are 613 laws in the Torah about all aspects of life. Among them are the **Ten Commandments**. These God-given laws, though basically for Jews, have influenced Christians as well. They are the rules that people must follow, according to God's holy law. The Ten Commandments have greatly influenced the laws and duties of generations of people, right up to the present day. They can be divided into two. First, the religious duties:

- *I am the Lord your God.*
- *You must have no other gods besides me.*
- *You must not use the name of the Lord, your God without reason.*
- *Remember to keep the Sabbath day holy; and on it you must not do any work.*

Second, the social duties:

- *Respect your father and your mother.*
- *You must not murder.*
- *You must not commit adultery.*
- *You must not steal.*
- *You must not give false evidence against your neighbour.*
- *You must not desire your neighbour's house, wife, nor anything that belongs to him.* (Exodus 20: 1–14)

Photo A

Photo B

22

KEY QUESTION

Can the Ten Commandments be applied to our modern world?

THINKING POINT

'You shall love your neighbour as you love yourself.'

(Leviticus 19: 18)

The Sermon on the Mount

At the heart of Jesus' teachings is the **Sermon on the Mount**. Jesus gave his sermon on a hillside, by the sea of Galilee in Palestine. He spoke to the ordinary folk – the farmers, tradesmen and fishermen.

In His sermon Jesus tried to show what life could be like if people could change the way they think and feel and act. He wasn't concerned with giving a set of rules or laws. He tried to give people a **vision of an ideal**. This means, He showed people how much better they *could* become, if they changed themselves.

The Sermon on the Mount is about trying to change the way people usually think, feel and act. We are not as different today from the farmers and fishermen of 2000 years ago as we sometimes think. If we look at some of Jesus' ideas, we can see that they can be applied to our situation today.

● *'Happy are those who work for peace; God will call them His children.'* *(Matthew 5: 9)*

● *'When someone asks you for something, give it to them.'* *(Matthew 5: 42)*

● *'Love your enemies ...'* *(Matthew 5: 44)*

● *'You must be perfect, just as your Father in heaven is perfect.'* *(Matthew 5: 48)*

● *'No one can be a slave of two masters; he will hate one and love the other; or he will*

be loyal to one and despise the other. You cannot serve both God and money.'

(Matthew 6: 24)

● *'And why worry about clothes? Look how the wild flowers grow; they do not work or make clothes for themselves. But I tell you that not even King Solomon with all his wealth had clothes as beautiful as one of these flowers. It is God who clothes the wild grass – grass that is here today and gone tomorrow, burnt up in the oven. Won't He be all the more sure to clothe you?'*

(Matthew 6: 28–30)

● *'Do not judge others, so that God will not judge you.'* *(Matthew 7: 1)*

● *'Why do you see the speck that is in your brother's eye, but do not notice the log that is in your own eye?'* *(Matthew 7: 3)*

THINGS TO DO

Look at the following ideas. Write down the part of the Sermon on the Mount that refers to them. For example, 'Try not to be greedy for money and material things' relates to 'You cannot serve both God and money.'

1 Try not to judge people.

2 Aim to be a perfect person.

3 Try to be caring even to those people you don't like.

4 Try to work for peace.

5 Try to be generous.

KEY IDEA

In His teachings Jesus encouraged people to aim for ideals – to make themselves better people.

11 IDEALS AND HEROES ● ● ● ● ● ● ● ● ● ● ● ●

What is an ideal?

'An ideal is an imaginary model of perfection.'

(*Concise English Dictionary*)

In other words it's something higher – something that we try to aim for. It's some sort of perfection that we try to work towards.

In the New Testament, Christians find an example of an ideal person in Jesus. For Christians this ideal is something they try to work towards. If we study the life of Jesus we find examples of this ideal.

He didn't judge people on the grounds of sex, race or religion.

He forgave His enemies. On the cross, when He was experiencing terrible agony, he said, *'Father forgive them.'* (*Luke 23: 34*).

He was very brave – He went to Jerusalem knowing that His enemies planned to have Him killed, and throughout His life He showed great love to everyone He came into contact with.

The Beatitudes

Here are some words which Jesus used in the Sermon on the Mount (see Unit 10). The ideals He mentions are in **bold**.

*'Happy are those who are **humble**; they will receive what God has promised.'*   (*Matthew 5: 5*)

*'Happy are those who are **merciful to others**; God will be merciful to them.'*   (*Matthew 5: 7*)

*'Happy are those who **work for peace**; God shall call them His children.'*   (*Matthew 5: 9*)

When we see a 'hero' in a film, they often show qualities such as bravery, forgiveness and loving kindness. Now, although we might not be able to live in such a way ourselves, we all wish that we could be a little braver, a little wiser, a little more clever, a little more forgiving, a little less jealous, a little less mean, a little less bad-tempered. All of us are trying to reach some sort of ideal.

THINGS TO DO

What is it that plays the most important role in the guidance of your conduct? Here are some possibilities. Your job is to rank them in order of importance to you, giving a 1 to what you think plays the most important role in guiding your behaviour, followed by a 2, and so on. (You can give the same number to more than one alternative.)

(a)   my attitudes towards other people

(b)   my ideals

(c)   my hopes

(d)   my desires

(e)   my appetites

(f)   my feelings

(g)   rules imposed on me by others

(h)   laws

(i)   my interests

(j)   my dislikes

(k)   my preferences

(l)   traditions I accept

(m)   my intelligence

(n)   money

(o)   science

(p)   the views of my friends

(q)   the views of my family

(r)   the views of my teachers

We've all got heroes. These days many of our ideal people come from TV, films, magazines or pop music. It is difficult to imagine it, but probably many of the people who are your heroes today might not still be when you're, say, 25. In fact, one day when you have children they will probably never have heard of some of today's heroes.

It could be said that there are **three types of heroes:**

1   Fashionable heroes who soon become forgotten.

2   Heroes whose name dies soon after they do.

3   Heroes whose names live on.

TASKS

1 Work in pairs. Write down the names of four people whom you consider to be your heroes.

2 Ask your partner to give them a mark (1, 2 or 3) to fit in with the three types of heroes.

3 How many points have your heroes been given?

4 Discuss your heroes and your marks with your partner.

5 Now write down the reasons why you chose these people to be your heroes.

6 Look at the following list of qualities. Mark your heroes according to this list.

1 Good looks

2 Good voice

3 Good dancer or sportsperson

4 Clever

5 Peace loving

6 Wise

7 Works for others

8 Kind and gentle

9 Courageous

10 Sacrificed their lives for others.

Hero profile

Martin Luther King (1929–68) dedicated his life to working for equal rights for black people in the United States of America. They had been torn from their homes in Africa to become slaves. Even in Martin Luther King's day they were treated as second-class citizens.

Despite many threats against his life Dr King organized various forms of peaceful protest to try to make the authorities give black people equal rights. He was awarded the Nobel Peace Prize in 1964 and, thanks to his leadership and inspiration, equal voting rights were given to black people in 1965. In

Dr Martin Luther King

1968, Martin Luther King was shot dead. He was only 39. His words, however, live on:

'If a man hasn't discovered something he will die for, he isn't fit to live.'

'Together we must learn to live as brothers, or together we will be forced to perish as fools.'

'I have a dream that my four little children will one day live in a nation where they will not be judged by the colour of their skin, but by the sort of people they are.'

THINKING POINT

'The greatest love a person can have for his friends is to give his life for them.'

(Jesus in John 15: 13)

12 THE GOLDEN RULE

Although the great religions of the world have developed in different parts of the world and at different times, they have much in common. For instance, if we look at seven of the great world religions, we find that they all teach that we should **treat others as we ourselves would like to be treated**. This rule, common to all religions, is known as the **Golden Rule**. This rule is very important. If people would live by it the world would be a much better place.

GROUP WORK

1 In small groups of three or four, discuss how you might feel if:

● *A person keeps staring at you*

● *Two people are saying horrible things about you in front of you*

● *A person keeps interrupting you when you speak*

● *Somebody hits you for no reason.*

2 If you decided to treat other people as you'd like to be treated, do you think you could ever do any of these things to somebody else?

3 Discuss some of the problems that exist in the world today. Write them down. Now try to work out how these problems might be solved if the Golden Rule was applied to them. Elect a spokesperson to explain the findings of your group to the rest of the class.

Buddhism	'I will act towards others exactly as I would act towards myself.' *From Udana-Varga* **c. 500 BCE**
Hinduism	'This is the sum of duty: Do naught to others Which, if done to thee, could cause thee pain.' *From The Mahabharata* **c. 150 BCE**
Christianity	'Treat others as you would like them to treat you.' *From Luke: Revised Standard Version of the New Testament* **c. 90 CE**
Judaism	'What is harmful to yourself do not to your fellow men. That is the whole of the law and the remainder is but commentary.' *From Hillel: The Talmud* **c. 100 CE**
Islam	'None of you 'truly' believe, until he wishes for his brothers what he wishes for himself.' *A saying of Prophet Muhammad recorded by accepted narrator al-Bukari* **7th century CE**
Sikhism	'As thou deemest thyself, so deem others.' 'Cause suffering to no one; Thereby return to your True Home with honour' *From Guru Granth Sahib* **1604 CE**
Bahá'í faith	'He should not wish for others that which he doth not wish for himself.' *From writings of Bahá'u'lláh* **c. 1870 CE**

Millions of homeless children around the world live in terrible conditions

This house was burnt in a racist attack

*F*OR DISCUSSION

● *In groups of four discuss what the Golden Rule means.*

● *Why do you think it has been called the 'Golden Rule'?*

*P*HOTO SCAN

Look at the two photographs. Explain in your own words what you scc. What might happen if the Golden Rule was applied in these two dreadful situations?

*T*HINGS TO DO

Design a poster for your bedroom using some of the ideas you've talked about today.

13 RELATIONSHIPS •••••••••••••••••••••

The word **relationship** simply means how we link with one another, or how we respond and react to each other. To **relate** to someone suggests that we have begun to trust or have a sense of respect for them.

Different kinds of relationships

We form relationships with people in many different ways and also on different levels. Some relationships are very important to us, e.g. with members of our family and close friends. These are **intimate** (or **primary**) relationships, and if these go wrong it can cause us great unhappiness. We rely on these people to support us and back us up.

We also form relationships with people who play less important roles in our lives, such as friends of the family or teachers at school. It is, however, necessary that we get along with these people who form **secondary** relationships, as they can influence and shape our lives.

> ## Key idea
> If relationships go wrong they can cause us great unhappiness.

We have different relationships within the family, too. Our relationships with our mother and father are the most important as they provide a sense of security. They are usually the first adults who influence our lives.

In some relationships we find ourselves in a **dominant** (top dog) position which can give us a sense of our own importance, for instance being the eldest child in a family where there are younger brothers and sisters. In this family situation the younger child **trusts** the older child; the younger child 'looks up' to the elder child for guidance. However, when the elder child goes out into the world, e.g. at school, they are no longer in this privileged position and meet with other people who think they are top dogs.

Changing relationships

When we were babies our relationship with others, especially our parents, was one of **dependency** (we needed them to do almost everything for us). As we grow up we learn that those around us also have needs, and we learn to give to each other instead of always taking. Then we become **interdependent** – we begin to rely on each other.

Difficulties in relationships might sometimes be painful, but they are necessary in order that we allow each other to change and develop. Understanding each other requires **mutual respect** (respecting each other) and allowing people to express themselves (to say, act and feel the way they want to).

Our relationships are always changing. We have to **adapt** or change ourselves, when situations change.

> ## For discussion
> Read the following account by a twelve year old boy, showing how his life situation changed and how he came to terms with it.
>
> *'When I was ten, my mum and dad split up. When they told me they were going to split up I was very upset. Fortunately, my mum and dad are very good friends now, and I like my mum's new boyfriend very much. I see my dad nearly every day but some people aren't so lucky. My friend Eddy – his mum and dad hate each other and he hardly ever sees his dad. More and more people these days are divorced and it can be very difficult for the children. I've drawn a chart showing what children can think.'* (Jamie, aged twelve)
>
> Feeling guilty that it was all my fault.
>
> Feeling that I may never see my dad very much.
>
> **CHILD'S POINT OF VIEW**
>
> Feeling scared that mum couldn't manage.
>
> Feeling everything has gone wrong.

Some relationships are very important

Respectfully Yours

In the past children have been told to respect their elders, as if adults should automatically have the respect of children. In most situations, respect has to be earned. Do you think an adult ought to be automatically respected by a child? How do you think people can earn each other's respect?

The world religions all teach that we should treat each other with respect. Relationships are seen as being very important because a person is judged, not by what they look like, or own, or where they come from, but by how they treat each other.

THINKING POINTS

Buddhism
'Let a man avoid evil deeds as a man who lives life avoids poison.'
(Buddha, in the *Dhamanpada 123*)

Christianity
'Love your neighbour as you love yourself.'
(Jesus, in *Matthew 22: 39*)

Judaism
'Don't plan anything that will hurt your neighbour.'
(*Proverbs 3: 29*)

ROLE PLAY – Improving relationships

KEY WORD
Compromise: accepting each other's point of view and reaching a solution, bending the rule.

Get into groups of three and act out the following situation. One person should be the son or daughter and the other two the parents.

Situation
There is a disco. The youngster is twelve years old and is allowed to be out until 10.30 p.m. on special occasions if their parents know where they are, and how they are getting home. The disco finishes at 11.30 p.m. and the youngster wants to stay until the end.

Son or daughter's case
'I'm going with friends that you know and like. You know my friends are OK and sensible. I can come to no harm. It's a very special occasion and it won't be repeated. The others are allowed to stay until 11.30. Why not me? Don't you trust me?'

The parents' case
'You must stand by the rules – 10.30 is late enough. If we let you go this time then you will want to go out until later next time. It's not a matter of trust. We trust you but you are only twelve years old.'

Using the cases as a guideline, try to find a **compromise** which allows a new understanding between the child and the parents which builds on **reasoning** and trust (respect for one another).

THINGS TO DO
Being a diplomat
Invent your own situation to illustrate the difficulties of a threesome. One of the three has a spare ticket to a concert. Both of the others would like to go. Find a solution to this problem.

14 FRIENDSHIP AND LOYALTY ••••••••

Friendship is an important part of all our lives. Loneliness is a very sad thing indeed. However, as we all know, friendships are not always easy. We sometimes argue with our friends. Friendships don't always last. The friends you have today may not be the friends you have in ten years' time. We have some friends who we feel closer to than others. We might even have some friends who, if we think about it, we don't really like very much.

In this section you will explore some ideas about friendship.

FOR YOUR FOLDERS

Try to write an answer to each of these questions. If possible give reasons for your replies.

1 Could a person be unreliable and still be your friend?

2 Could a person be untrustworthy, and still be your friend?

3 Could a person be cruel, and still be your friend?

4 Could a person be unhappy, and still be your friend?

5 Could a person be insensitive, and still be your friend?

6 Could a person refuse to lend you things, and still be your friend?

7 Could a person be vulgar, and still be your friend?

8 Could a person be weak, and still be your friend?

9 What three features would you most like a friend of yours to have?

10 Would you say that you also have these features?

11 What three features would you not like your friend to have?

12 Do you have any of these features?

13 Complete the following sentence by choosing some of the phrases from the columns below, or by using a phrase of your own:

My friends are people ...

(a) I like

(b) who like me

(c) I go out with

(d) I'm acquainted with

(e) I love

(f) who love me

(g) I know

(h) I feel comfortable with

(i) I trust

(j) I tell my thoughts to

(k) who tell me private things

(l) who won't let me down

(m) who count on me.

'The only way to have a friend is to be one.'

THINKING POINTS

'Some friendships do not last, but some friends are more loyal than brothers.'

(Proverbs 18: 24)

'The only way to have a friend is to be one.'

(Emerson, American writer)

'The greatest love a person can have for his friends is to give his life for them.'

(Jesus, in John 15: 1)

FOR DISCUSSION

1 Is every person you like your friend?

2 Are there people you like who are not your friends?

3 Are only people you *like* your friends?

4 Your friend has just bought a new jacket. She is thrilled with it but you think it's horrible. When she says, 'What do you think of my beautiful jacket?', how would you reply?

5 Your friend has just been accused of breaking into the school sports hall and stealing some footballs. He says he was nowhere near the sports hall but was playing with you. This isn't true. Do you protect your friend or tell the truth?

6 You see your friend bullying a younger child. What do you do?

Loyalty

FOR YOUR FOLDERS

1 Do you agree or disagree with the following descriptions of loyalty? In each case, give your reasons.

(a) Loyalty is keeping your word of honour.

(b) Loyalty is being faithful to your oath.

(c) Loyalty is being faithful to your government.

(d) Loyalty is obeying the law.

(e) Loyalty is not breaking your promises.

2 Write down what you think loyalty means.

FOR DISCUSSION

Is loyalty a two-way thing? Give reasons for your answers.

1 Is it right for friends to be loyal to each other?

2 Is it right for married people to be loyal to each other, or is it all right for one to be loyal but not the other?

3 Is it right for class mates to be loyal to one another?

4 Is it right for brothers and sisters to be loyal to one another?

5 Is it right for children to be loyal to their parents, but unnecesary for parents to be loyal to their children?

6 Is it right for children to be loyal to their pets, but permissable for their pets not to be loyal to them?

7 Is it right for citizens to be loyal to their government, but okay if their government is not loyal to them?

8 Can you be loyal to your natural environment?

15 HAPPY FAMILIES? ● ● ● ● ● ● ● ● ● ● ● ● ● ● ● ●

Families are found in every country in the world and in every age throughout history. Every family is different. The image of the 'ideal' family that we see in advertisements is very different from most people's experiences of the family. When a group of people live very closely together there are bound to be some problems.

TASK 1
Read these extracts from a teenage problem page. Imagine you are the editor of the problem page, and try to write answers to the unanswered letters B and C.

The atmosphere at home gets me down. My brother stays out all night sometimes and Mum and Dad can't stop worrying about him. I think he might be in trouble with the police, and he gets drunk and yells at my mum. He used to be so nice but now he's wrecking his life, and the rest of the family's too. I still love him, but the rows are so bad I sometimes wish he'd leave.

It's awful to have to stand back and watch people you love argue and fight. Sometimes you can even start feeling guilty yourself just because there isn't anything you can do to help.

When you're young you always think of your family as one cosy little unit. When you're older you realize that they're all separate people who can lead separate lives. You can still love them but you can't stop them going their own way. What your brother decides to do is up to him, and in the meantime you can only help by giving him and your parents all the love and support you can. **A**

My brother is a year older than me and he bullies me all the time. He kicks, pinches and punches me but always where the bruises won't show; he calls me names and makes my life a misery. If I tell mum, she says, 'Ignore him.' If I try to stand up to him for myself I always get half the blame for the huge row that follows. I'm thirteen. **B**

My mum has recently remarried and my stepfather has moved in, along with his daughter from his first marriage. They're both nice and I don't mind Mum getting married, but I can't get used to them being around. I feel as if his daughter gets more attention from Mum than I do. When my first dad left it was just Mum and me for ages and we went through a lot together, but sometimes I think I was happier then. **C**

What does a family do?
● *It provides a safe community for having children and bringing them up.*
● *It forms the group in which most people spend most of their time.*
● *It helps us to learn acceptable ways to treat other people.*
● *It teaches us the customs and traditions of our society.*
● *It provides a place where the aged, the sick and disabled people can be cared for.*

Family life and the Bible
In the Bible there are references to the family.
'Honour your father and your mother.'
(Exodus 20: 12)
'Do not despise your mother when she is old.'
(Proverbs 23: 22)
In all His teachings Jesus said that human beings should love and care for each other. People should be treated with respect – as individuals in their own right.

Parenthood
Our parents, especially in our early years, are the most important people in the world. The way they treat us affects our whole life and their influence is enormous. Parents have the **right** and the **duty** to look after their own children. In the UK the law will not normally interfere unless it is thought that the child is not being properly cared for. If a marriage breaks up a court usually decides how these rights and duties are to be shared out.

Ill-treatment
It is a criminal offence to assault, ill-treat, neglect or abandon a child under the age of sixteen.

Punishment
Parents have the right to control the behaviour of their children and to punish them to a reasonable extent.

Education

Parents have a duty to make sure their children receive full-time education until they reach the school-leaving age.

Religion

Parents have the right to decide the religion in which a child should be brought up.

Medical treatment

Parents usually have the right to allow or forbid medical treatment for children under the age of sixteen. In some cases the courts have the power to decide, if they feel that the best interests of the child are being ignored.

Name

Parents can decide what their children shall be called.

Access

Parents have a legal right to see their children, whoever they are living with, unless the courts decide otherwise.

Property

Children can own property or money, and parents have no right to it.

> If you are personally concerned about any of these things you can call **Childline**: **0800 1111**.

TASK 2

Look at the advertisement for a parent. In pairs, discuss what you think it's trying to say. Now make up your own advertisement: 'Wanted – Ideal child'.

WANTED

Responsible person (male or female) needed to take on a lifelong project. Applicants must be willing to work 24 hours a day, seven days of the week. A few hours off after five years. An excellent knowledge of nutrition, education, child psychology, money matters and health care would be helpful. No experience is necessary. No training is given. You must be kind, humorous, loving, gentle, patient and energetic. This job is unpaid.

FOR YOUR FOLDERS

1 Explain in your own words what a family is, and what it does.

2 What problems exist in families?

3 How do you think some of these problems might be solved?

4 After reading the section on parenthood try to explain the difference between a right and a duty.

5 Why do you think it's not always easy to be a parent?

6 Why do you think it's not always easy being a child in a family?

7 Not everyone is lucky enough to have a family. What do you think life must be like without a family?

16 MARRIAGE ••••••••••••••••••••••••••••

At some time in their lives, most adult human beings get married. They find a partner, fall in love and decide they want to live with that person for the rest of their lives.

Marriage is an important part of life. When somebody decides to marry, they are making a **commitment** (a pledge, a promise). They are saying, 'We will be together for the rest of our lives.'

Why do people decide to marry? Here are just some reasons:

● *to share their lives in a close loving relationship*
● *to have children and bring them up in a happy family*
● *to have lifelong companionship*
● *to share their sexuality with each other over a lifetime.*

All the world religions set a high value on marriage. They all teach that it is part of God's plan for people to marry, and that marriage is the right relationship for people to make love and have children. Here are just some views.

A Buddhist view

Buddhists believe that within a marriage a couple can practise their religion, leading to great happiness. In the Dhammapada, the Buddha said:

'To support one's mother and father,
To care for one's wife and children,
And to have a peaceful occupation.
This is the highest blessing.'

A Christian view

Christians believe that in their love for each other, a married couple will experience and learn of God's love for His creation. In the Christian marriage service a couple promises to love and honour each other for the rest of their lives. They say:

'I take thee to be my wedded husband (or wife), to have and to hold, from this day forward, for better or worse, for richer, for poorer, in sickness and in health, to love and to cherish till death us do part, according to God's holy law ....'

(Book of Common Prayer)

A Hindu view

For a Hindu, marriage is a religious duty. Many Hindu parents arrange their children's marriages. They consider carefully the horoscopes of the young people, their personalities and the social, financial and religious position of both families.

A Jewish view

Jews believe that a happy marriage creates a good environment for raising a family. They believe that through marriage, men and women are able to develop as complete individuals. In the first book of the Torah it says:

'... a man leaves his father and mother and is united with his wife and they become one'.

(Genesis 2: 24)

A Muslim view

Muslims believe that finding a good life partner and building up a relationship together is a religious duty.

'Whoever gets married has completed half of his faith; therefore let him be conscious of Allah in the other half of his faith.'

(Hadith)

A Sikh view

For Sikhs, marriage is a religious act. They believe that God intended human beings to marry. In the Guru Granth Sahib it says:

'They are not man and wife who have only physical contact. Only those are truly married who have one spirit in two bodies.'

(Guru Granth Sahib, 788)

Indian women preparing for marriage

*I*N GROUPS

Me, married?

One day, you will probably decide to get married. It's an enormous decision. In groups of three or four, preferably boys and girls, discuss the following.

- *Couples should know each other inside out before they get married.*
- *Individuals should know themselves before they get married.*
- *Couples should keep their own hobbies.*
- *Having children puts great pressure on a couple's relationship.*
- *People would be better off if older people arranged their marriages for them.*
- *Falling in love is only a short-term experience. Learning to love somebody, 'warts and all', takes a lifetime.*
- *People expect too much from marriage.*
- *Marriage is tough.*

Divorce

It is estimated that nearly one in three marriages in Britain end in divorce. When a couple splits up it can be a very painful emotional experience. This is especially true when there are children involved. However, sometimes the children might be better off living with one parent than with two parents who are having terrible arguments.

There are many reasons why people get divorced. Here are just a few:

- *People change – the person who marries at 21 may be a different person at 30.*
- *Wrong expectations – people have very high hopes about marriage and can become disillusioned by the reality.*
- *Money problems and unemployment can add great stress to a relationship.*
- *Taking each other for granted – people stop talking and communicating and begin arguing over small things.*
- *People see marriage as being the end of a romantic relationship, but in fact it is just the beginning.*

FOR DISCUSSION

'It's better for the children's sake for two arguing parents to separate than to stay married.'

How do you feel about this statement? Do you agree or disagree?

17 BODY MATTERS ●●●●●●●●●●●●●●●●●●●

We've only got one body so we must take care of it. Often we take our bodies for granted. When we fall asleep at night we believe that our bodies will be fit and well in the morning, and ready for another day. It's only when we become ill, or are in pain, that we realize how important a healthy body is.

'Lead me not into temptation.'

When we're young we are often tempted to do some things that may not be very good for our bodies. Can you think of some things that aren't good for our bodies? Here are just a few ideas:

- *eating too much sugar*
- *eating too much salt*
- *staying up late*
- *smoking*
- *drinking lots of alcohol*
- *using drugs and solvents (see Unit 40).*

IN GROUPS

In groups of three or four discuss the following.

- *What things do I do that I know are bad for my body?*
- *Why do I do these things?*
- *Would I enjoy them if I could see what they are doing to my insides?*
- *Do other people sometimes force me to do these things?*
- *Why do I sometimes take my body for granted?*

There's no smoke without fire!

At some time in our lives somebody is going to tempt us to 'have a fag'. When young people first smoke cigarettes they hate them. They feel sick, go green and cough. But if they keep trying they can become smokers. What does it mean to be a smoker? People who smoke say, 'It'll never happen to me,' but here are just a few things that happen to ordinary people like you.

- *Every week, 1000 smokers die.*
- *Each cigarette takes five minutes off your life.*
- *Only six smokers in every 100 survive lung cancer.*
- *With every puff, 300 chemicals enter the blood stream.*
- *Several hundred non-smokers die in the UK each year as a result of* **passive smoking.**

THINGS TO DO

The majority of smokers begin smoking before the age of sixteen. Design an anti-smoking poster, aimed at your age group, using some of the facts on these pages.

PROJECT

Design a project on 'Temptation'. Include in it things like diet, smoking, drinking and solvent abuse.

Gather information from some of the following sources: the library, a doctor's surgery, health clinic, a hospital, your tutor, school textbooks.

Try to explain in your project what sort of things are bad for your body and why people are sometimes tempted to put these things in their bodies.

Growing up

Every human being does a lot of growing from the time when they're born to when they become adult. The human body changes in different ways at different times. Sometimes we may be embarrassed about our bodies. However, we must try to remember that:

- *Each one of us is different; we are all special.*
- *We come in all shapes and sizes and it would be a boring world if we all looked the same.*
- *We are all much more than just what we look like.*

- *Our bodies carry our 'real selves' around.*
- *Everybody is beautiful in their own way.*
- *Some time during the day, everyone should say to themselves, 'I enjoy the way I am.'*
- *If other people feel they must make fun of us, it's them who have the real problem, not us.*

A religious view

All the world religions teach that our bodies are very precious things and we should take care of them. They are a gift and, like anything that is given to us, we should take care of them.

'Surely you know that you are God's temple and that God's Spirit lives in you! So if anyone destroys God's temple, God will destroy him. For God's temple is holy, and you yourselves are his temple.'

(1 Corinthians 3 : 16–17)

The world religions also teach that each human being is far more than just a body, or how they look. Each person is given a **spirit** – something they can't see, but which is the true and lasting part of the person. The body will die but the spirit will live on.

Buddhists believe that this spirit is reborn many times and in many bodily forms. They believe that this life is a very special gift indeed. They believe we might have been born many times before we reached this life, and to live as human beings in this life is a precious gift. Because life is a gift we should look after ourselves as well as other beings, both human and animal. Buddhism, like all religions, teaches that what we do to our body affects our mind.

THINKING POINTS

'Health is the greatest of gifts.'

(Buddhist teaching, Dhammapada, 204)

What's in tobacco? Tobacco smoke contains nicotine which is addictive, tar which causes cancer, and carbon monoxide which contributes to strokes, heart disease and circulation problems.

FOR DISCUSSION

- *We are all special.*
- *Life is a gift.*
- *Our bodies are like vehicles; they carry the 'real me' around.*
- *I am not just how I look.*
- *My body affects my mind.*

18 THE BODY BEAUTIFUL? •••••••••••

In our society we are shown lots of images by the **media**. The media includes television, advertisements, newspapers and magazines. These images influence the way in which we think about ourselves and other people. Often these images are telling us that we will only be happy, attractive and successful in life if we look a certain way. In this section you will explore the effect these images have on us.

FOR DISCUSSION

- *Do you choose a friend because of the way they look?*
- *Do you wish you looked like somebody else? Why? Can you give reasons?*
- *Ideas about what is good-looking change from age to age. For example, in the 1920s women put bandages around their chests to give a flat-chested look, which was fashionable.*
- *'You can't judge a book by its cover.'*
- *People make loads of money by trying to sell us ideas about what is good-looking.*

IN GROUPS

Read this newspaper article. Discuss it in groups of three or four.

IS LIFE ABOUT LOOKING LIKE THIS?

First it was girls who were driven to eating disorders by glamorous images of models in magazines and on television. Now it seems that young men are suffering the same fate. More and more young people are becoming unhappy because of the way they look. Media images of hunks, 'gorgeous' young men and women models, put pressure on young people to look a certain way. Girls don't want to look fat. Boys don't want to look thin. Why can't we just let our young people be content and happy with the way they look?

If we look at the way things are advertised, we will find that advertisers often use the human body to sell their products. This has been especially true of women's bodies which have been most commonly used and abused in this way.

Women's bodies are used to sell fast cars, chocolates and newspapers. This is called **exploitation**. These images that are all around affect the way we think about the female body. The average person living in a city in Britain is bombarded by over 1600 advertising images a day. Many of these images are **sexist** – they treat women as objects.

IN GROUPS

In groups of four (two girls and two boys), discuss the following.

- *Adverts using women's bodies do not respect women.*
- *Adverts like this give boys false ideas about girls.*
- *In our society it's more important what a person looks like than what a person is actually like.*
- *The media confuse us about how we should treat other people.*
- *Newspapers which show women in half-undressed poses should be banned.*
- *There is far more to a person than just the way they look.*

THINKING POINTS

'Fools follow vanity.'

(Buddhist teaching, Dhammapada, 27)

'A good reputation is better than expensive perfume.'

(Ecclesiastes 7: 1)

Incredible hunks or incredible hulks?

How to lose pounds with cosmetic surgery

PHOTO SCAN

1   Look at the photograph of male strippers. It takes two hours in the gym each day to keep this look. Do you think it is worth it?

How would you describe the way they look? Have a brainstorm and write down some words that come to your mind when you look at the photograph. Discuss your findings with a member of the opposite sex.

A mother and child with a different kind of weight problem

2   Look at the advertisement for cosmetic surgery.

Liposuction involves sucking out fat from some parts of the body. Why would a woman consider going to such lengths? Sometimes these operations can be dangerous and are usually very painful. Do you think it is fair that women are pressurized into looking a certain way in our society?

3   This photograph was taken in the Sudan.

Do you think it is right that while our society is so obsessed with the way people look, people not very far away are struggling to stay alive?

19 RIGHT AND WRONG ••••••••••

In this section you will explore some ideas to do with right and wrong. Break up into groups of about ten and discuss the following questions. *Wherever possible try to give reasons for your comments.*

FOR DISCUSSION 1

- *Can something be unpleasant to do, and still be right? Give examples.*
- *Can something be pleasant to do, and still be wrong? Give examples.*
- *Can something be allowed, and still be wrong? Give examples.*
- *Can something be forbidden, and still be right? Give examples.*

FOR DISCUSSION 2

- *Is it possible that some people do things which they call 'right', and yet those things they do are really harmful to other people?*
- *Is it possible that some people do things which almost no one thinks are right, and yet which are really very helpful to everyone?*
- *Is it possible that some things are wrong to do, even if doing them doesn't hurt anyone?*
- *Is it possible that some things are right to do, even though some people get hurt as a result?*
- *Is it possible that some things are neither right nor wrong to do?*
- *Is it possible that some things are always right, and other things are always wrong?*
- *Is it possible that, if it's wrong for everyone else to do certain things, it's also wrong for you?*
- *Is it possible that certain things may be wrong for another person to do, but right for you?*
- *Is it possible that sometimes other people know what you should do better than you know it?*
- *Is it possible that sometimes you know what you should do better than anyone else?*

IN PAIRS

Look at the following case studies. Discuss what you think the person should do in each case.

Case study 1

John is fifteen. He lives in a high-rise block of flats with his mum and five young brothers and sisters. They are very poor, and often have very little to eat. Some of John's friends say they'll give him £500 if he keeps watch while they burgle a shop.

Case study 2

Melanie is thirteen. Her friends want her to come and watch an '18' film. Melanie's parents do not want their daughter watching such a film. Melanie doesn't want to upset her parents or fall out with her friends. The only way she can get to the pictures is to lie to her parents.

Case study 3

Two bullies at school keep poking fun at Mark who has got a lisp. Mark's best friend Joey has told the teacher about the bullies, but they continue to tease Mark. Joey is a good boxer and he is tempted to sort out the two bullies.

Case study 4

Les is fourteen. He goes out a lot and likes spending money on clothes, sweets and the cinema. He is offered work one day a week by an older friend. It will bring him £30, but it means missing a day at school.

What reasons do you think these people might give for arguing that it is right to kill another human being?

Right thinking

Actions begin with thoughts. If we think about somebody or something in a bad way we are likely to behave in a bad way. All of the world religions teach that as well as trying to change our outward actions we should also try to change our inner thoughts.

This is not easy. Our thoughts often come flooding in like a great river. We can be thinking of something one moment and of something totally different the next. It is true to say that *our thoughts think us.* Often we are not in control of them. Because of this, when something happens to us we just **react** – we do something or say something before we even know what we've done.

All of the world religions teach that some time during the day we should just stop and become quiet inside. These exercises are called prayer, meditation and contemplation. By doing this we can give our thoughts a rest from their constant wanderings, and perhaps prepare ourselves for the day, so we do not react quite so much.

20 CONSEQUENCES ●●●●●●●●●●●●●●●●●●●●

When we try to work out what is the right or wrong thing to do, we often find that things aren't always straightforward. Sometimes it is easy to know what is the right or wrong thing to do; at other times it is not. As we grow up we begin to discover what is right and wrong. Some of the ways we discover these things are:

by consequence
If I do such and such a thing, this is likely to happen.

by example
Watching how other people behave and copying them.

by experience
If you do something, you find out what happens. This will affect what you do in the future.

by following rules
Many rules have been made to try to protect people.

by your feelings
If somebody hurts me I may (or may not) hurt somebody else because I know what it feels like.

*I*N GROUPS

When we make decisions about what to do we have to ask ourselves the following questions.

1 How will my decision affect me?
2 How will my decision affect my family or friends?
3 How will my decision affect my community?
4 How will my decision affect the world?

In groups of four or five discuss the following situations. What would you decide to do regarding them? Answer the four questions above after you've made your decision.

● *Your best mate has started smoking. He tries to convince you to smoke, telling you that it's 'cool to smoke'.* ➤

● *You have a Saturday morning job in a shop. A good friend asks if she can buy a magazine. As you get it for her, you notice her putting a bar of chocolate from the counter into her pocket.*
● *On Monday, you find a twenty pound note outside the post office. You know it's pension day because your gran goes to the post office on a Monday.*
● *Ten bullies keep on picking on your best mate. You know the parents of one of the bullies.*

Now report back your findings to the rest of the class.

Long-term consequences

Sometimes when somebody does something, the consequences of that action can stay with that person for the rest of their life. It is very important that we think about long-term consequences, because a wrong action or decision can ruin lives. Here are just two tragic examples.

Example one

When John was sixteen he borrowed his friend's motorbike. He began showing off on it and overtaking on bends. He did it once too often, and fell off at 145 kph. John is now in a wheelchair – paralysed from the waist down.

Example two

When Tracey was sixteen she got very drunk at a party. She ended up sleeping with an older man she didn't know. A few months later she began feeling ill and was diagnosed HIV positive. She is now 18 with full-blown AIDS (see Unit 38).

As well as having to make decisions as individuals, we have to make important decisions as a group. There are also decisions that have to be made by the Government and by the Law. In these following extracts two young people present their views as to whether raves should be banned or not.

Viewpoint 1   Ravin' mad

'The drug Ecstasy is widely available at many raves. It leads young people to experiment with drugs. At least six people have died from taking Ecstasy at raves. Organizers use land that doesn't belong to them for these raves – trespassing on other people's property. These raves are a real health risk – they often take place in old warehouses which could easily catch fire. People living nearby have to put up with loud music, heavy traffic and noisy people, until the early hours of the morning. The raves are really difficult to control, and it costs the police lots of time and money to try to control them.'

(Alison, aged seventeen)

Viewpoint 2   Keep ravin'...

'If you stop raves you won't stop people taking drugs. Only a small number of party goers take drugs. Most go for the music and the atmosphere. If raves were banned you wouldn't stop them – people would organize their own illegal raves, and the problems between young people and the police would get worse. Anyway, young people have always loved going to parties   that's all that raves are, just big parties. It's part of our society and rave music has earnt a lot of money for this country.'

(Rob, aged sixteen)

Dancing at a rave

FOR YOUR FOLDERS

Imagine you are a judge and you have to make a decision about whether raves ought to be banned. Read the two viewpoints and answer the following questions.

1 What do you think are the possible consequences of banning raves?

2 Would you ban raves? Give reasons for your answer.

3 All the world religions teach the Golden Rule (see Unit 12). If this rule was applied to the question of whether raves ought to be banned, what do you think would be the outcome?

Children's rights

It is widely agreed that children have **rights**. In 1959 the United Nations presented the **Declaration of the Rights of the Child.** This aimed to make governments make new laws, or strengthen the existing laws, to protect children. The full rights are listed below.

All children should be equally entitled to the following rights.

- *A child should be able to grow and develop in healthy surroundings.*
- *From birth, a child should have the right to a name and nationality.*
- *A child should be protected before and after birth, and should have enough food, medical help and places to live and play.*
- *Any handicapped child should have special treatment, education and care.*
- *A child needs love and understanding and should be brought up by people who can give the child affection and security.*
- *A child should be able to have free education. All children should have the opportunity to develop their abilities, their judgement and their sense of responsibility.*
- *In any event, children should be among the first people to be helped and protected.*
- *Children should be protected from neglect and cruelty and from people who might take advantage of them. There should be an age limit for starting work. The type of work should not affect a child's development, health or education.*
- *All children should be treated equally and brought up to care for and value other people.*

A child should be able to grow and develop in healthy surroundings. Sadly, millions of children in the world grow up in absolute poverty

These rights might seem to be common sense. However, in the past children were often treated very badly. Indeed, in many parts of the world today, children are still treated very badly. For instance, millions of children around the world work as slaves. In India alone there are an estimated 44 million child slaves.

> ## THINKING POINTS
>
> *'It would be better for him if a millstone were hung around his neck and he were cast into the sea, than that he should cause one of these little ones to stumble.'*
>
> (Jesus, in Luke 17: 2)
>
> *'Your children are not your children.*
> *They are the sons and daughters*
> *of Life's longing for itself.*
> *They come through you but not from you,*
> *and though they are with you yet they belong not to you.*
> *You may give them your love but not your thoughts.*
> *For they have their own thoughts ...*
> *You may strive to be like them*
> *but seek not to make them like you ...'*
>
> (Kahlil Gibran, The Prophet)

FOR YOUR FOLDERS

1 Young people spend a large part of their life in schools. Read the following and then explain in a sentence if you think you have a right to:

(a) privacy, with regard to your desk and locker

(b) select your own teachers

(c) wear anything you want to school

(d) stay home when it rains

(e) never be suspended from school

(f) be treated with respect at all times in school

(g) remain silent in class

(h) talk in class

(i) write graffiti on the school walls

(j) change school ideas.

2 What do you think are the responsibilities you have towards:

(a) yourself

(b) your family

(c) your friends

(d) your neighbours

(e) your community?

Poverty and rights

Thousands of children are spending their lives in bed and breakfast accommodation. Often their parents are homeless, from ethnic minority groups, lone mothers, or those who speak little or no English, such as refugees or immigrant families.

Pauline, who has ten children, spent two years in a one bedroom flat.

'If the school sent them home with a book to read out loud, you couldn't listen to them read because it might wake up the baby. In the flat you had to climb over beds to get into bed; sleep was the last thing they got. The girls would start their homework and then the baby would crawl all over them or the boys would want the television on.'

KEY QUESTION

How does poverty affect children's rights?

Where do rights come from?

Here are three viewpoints.

'All human beings are special. We are not here on this earth by chance. We are here for a reason. When God created this planet He wanted human beings to take care of the world and everything in it. Because of this we have responsibilities and we have rights to make sure everyone is treated with respect.'

(Clare, aged fourteen)

'Human beings like to be together. We live together and because of this we have to have rights so that we can survive together.'

(Tom, aged thirteen)

'Because we are able to think, we can think about what other people are going through. So we have an idea of human rights to help us.'

(Lucy, aged fourteen)

FOR DISCUSSION

● *'With rights come responsibilities.'*
● *'Some people have more rights than others.'*
● *'Children should be given more rights in school.'*

22 REVERENCE FOR LIFE ●●●●●●●●●●●●●●

A young person who watches about twenty hours of television every week will have seen around 18 000 screen deaths by the time they are fourteen years old. Some people may argue that this is not a problem. However, some people feel that young people are having their 'reverence for life' taken away.

KEY QUESTION

Do we often forget that we live on a beautiful planet?

Life is a precious gift. Think of your own life. Think of your hopes, ideas, feelings, loved ones, joys, sadness, excitement, fun and hobbies. Everybody's life is full of such things. In many ways we are not so very different from each other.

Yet human beings hurt each other and harm the planet. Despite the fact that we are similar, some people do not honour and respect other people. More than this, human beings do not honour and respect other forms of life on this planet.

Albert Schweitzer (1875–1965) was a medical missionary in Africa and a Christian thinker. He believed that the most important thing we can have is reverence for life. All our behaviour should come from a deep understanding of the gift of life. He wrote:

'Reverence concerning all life is the greatest commandment ... we take this so slightly, thoughtlessly plucking a flower, thoughtlessly stepping on a poor insect, thoughtlessly disregarding the suffering and lives of our fellow men and women.'

Schweitzer believed that there was a 'terrible blindness' in our world. We cannot see that life is a wonderful, precious and mysterious gift. We watch people starving to death on our televisions. We spend millions upon millions of pounds making films about murder, war, violence, when we could be making a better world. We forget that these moving pictures that flicker on our screens are real people with feelings and thoughts like us. We forget that while we sit and watch a horror movie millions of people are living in a nightmare world. We want to be entertained. They want food, clothes and shelter. We want the latest computer toy. They want justice.

At the root of all religious teachings, lies the idea that life is sacred and should be revered. All world religions teach that all life is a gift from God, hence all life is sacred.

THINGS TO DO

1 Sacred means many things: holy, whole, precious, special, divine, beautiful, mysterious, hallowed.

   Look these words up in a dictionary. Write down some of the meanings that you find. Now try to write a poem about 'The Sacred'.

2 What is reverence for life? The word 'reverence' means things like hallow, veneration, honour, respect. Look up these words in a dictionary to find out what they mean.

Our planet is a beautiful and precious home

THINKING POINTS

'We need to affirm the sacredness of all human life. Every person is somebody because he is a child of God.'

(Martin Luther King)

'Thou shalt not kill.'

(Exodus 20: 13)

'All breathing, existing, living sentient creatures should not be slain, or treated with violence, nor abused, nor tormented, nor driven away.'

(Buddhist Scriptures, Anchoranga Sutra, 2300 BCE)

'Teach your children what we have taught our children, that the earth is our Mother. Whatever befalls the earth befalls the sons of the earth. If men spit upon the ground, they spit upon themselves. This we know – the earth does not belong to man, man belongs to the earth. All things are connected like the blood which unites one family. Whatever befalls the earth befalls the sons of the earth. Man did not weave the web of life; he is merely a strand in it. Whatever he does to the web, he does to himself ... to harm the earth is to heap contempt on its creator.'

(Chief Seattle, Native American Indian Chief)

If the Earth
were only a few feet in diameter,
floating a few feet above a field somewhere,
people would come from everywhere to marvel
at it. People would walk around it marvelling at its
big pools of water, its little pools and the water flowing
between. People would marvel at the bumps on it and the
holes in it. They would marvel at the very thin layer of gas
surrounding it and the water suspended in the gas. The people
would marvel at all the creatures walking around the surface of
the ball and at the creatures in the water. The people would
declare it as sacred because it was the only one, and they would
protect it so that it would not be hurt. The ball would be the
greatest wonder known, and people would come to pray to
it, to be healed, to gain knowledge, to know beauty and to
wonder how it could be. People would love it and defend
it with their lives because they would somehow
know that their lives could be nothing
without it. If the Earth were only
a few feet in diameter.

Joe Miller

FOR DISCUSSION

- 'We are losing respect for life.'
- 'We are blind to the suffering of others.'
- 'Life is a mysterious gift.'

KEY IDEA

Life is a gift.
We live on a beautiful planet and we need to try and open our eyes to the beauty around us.

23 ANOTHER PERSON'S SHOES········

When something horrible happens to us, we know how it feels. We know how it hurts. Pain can be either **physical** (our bodies hurt) or it can be **psychological** (our feelings hurt).

However, it is not always easy to feel somebody else's pain or hurt. We often can see the effects (for example, somebody might cry or be very upset), but we don't know how it actually **feels**. Or do we?

One part of being human means that we can imagine what it's like to be somebody else. We might never know exactly how it feels to be somebody else, but we have some idea, because we can imagine how we'd feel if we were in their situation.

We have seen that all the world religions teach the Golden Rule (see Unit 12) – that we should treat people the same way as we'd like to be treated. This means that we should try to imagine how we'd like to be treated and then try to treat other people in the same way. We should try to imagine what it would be like to be in somebody else's situation, to put ourselves in somebody else's shoes.

Today, thanks to satellites, newspapers and television, we are able to sit down at home and watch pictures from all over the world. Some of these pictures can be very upsetting. The world seems to be an unhappy place for millions of people. Because of violence and greed many people suffer. Some people think that although these pictures of the victims of starvation, pollution or war **inform** us (tell us what's happening in the world), they also make us **insensitive** (they stop us feeling). We get so used to seeing these helpless victims that we forget that they are like us, and have feelings as well.

Like us, they have families, dreams, hopes and plans. Often it is too easy to forget that, and just to think of these people as being helpless victims and not human beings like us.

This is also sometimes true of people we know. If we hurt them or are cruel to them, we often forget that they are like us. We forget to ask ourselves the question, 'How would I feel if I was in his or her position?'

PHOTO SCAN

Spend exactly one minute looking at each photograph in this section. Now answer the following questions in your folders.

1 What do you think has happened to the people in the photograph?

2 What thoughts might be going through these people's head?

3 How do you think each person will be feeling about the situation?

4 How do you think the people will be feeling about the future?

5 How might the people's families feel?

6 How do you think the people who caused this suffering will be feeling? Would they feel any different if they saw this photograph?

7 How do you think you'd be feeling if you were in these people's situations?

8 What do you think your thoughts might be if you were in these people's situations?

9 What do you think you could do to stop such terrible things happening?

10 Why do you think we all have problems about putting ourselves in another person's situation?

11 If everyone in the world could feel exactly as the people in the photographs feel for just one minute, do you think awful things like this might stop? Give reasons for your answer.

12 Now stop and look at the photographs again. Spend another minute studying each photograph. Try hard to imagine that you are a person in one of the photographs. Write down some words that you think describe how this person feels. If you can, using these words, try to write a poem entitled 'Please listen to me ....'

There are many thousands of people in Cambodia who have been disabled, made homeless and hungry or orphaned because of the war. People are still today having their limbs blown off by land mines

A column of Bosnian Muslim amputees moves through Srebrenica in the former Yugoslavia

KEY IDEA

Every human being on earth has feelings, hopes and dreams. We need sometimes to ask ourselves the question, 'How would I feel if I was in their shoes?'

24 PREJUDICE •••••••••••••••••••••••••••••

There are many things to learn. A famous psychiatrist called R. D. Laing once said, *'Everything we know is less than what there is'.*

Stereotyping

Often, when people don't understand something, they tend to **stereotype** it. This means that they fix an idea of something or someone into a mould which they're not prepared to change. They insist that this mould is the only possible one.

A stereotype comes out of ignorance. When we don't really know about someone or something, we can get a fixed idea in our heads and think of these people or things in a fixed way.

Often people in one country will stereotype people from another country. They'll say things like:

- *'All Welshmen are rugby players.'*
- *'All Scotsmen wear kilts.'*
- *'All French people eat garlic.'*

These are some of the gentler types of stereotypes. There are other stereotypes that are very cruel.

Stereotypes are fixed ideas. They put all people into little boxes, or compartments. We can see from the examples of stereotypes above that they are false. Some Welshmen have never played rugby. Very few Scotsmen wear kilts, and not all French people eat garlic.

Stereotypes can be very dangerous too. In Germany in the 1930s, the ruling party under Adolf Hitler stereotyped all Jewish people. It had fixed ideas about the Jews and these ideas resulted in six million Jews being murdered in the Nazi concentration camps.

> ### KEY IDEA
> Stereotyping comes from ignorance.

The Jews were used as **scapegoats**. A scapegoat is somebody who is blamed, although they are usually innocent. In Nazi

Jews were used as scapegoats in Nazi Germany

Germany the Jews were blamed for the terrible unemployment and inflation. Often, we as individuals blame other people if things go wrong.

Stereotypes are built on **prejudices**. A prejudice is a feeling or an attitude that people develop about certain types of people, before they have had personal experiences of them. Stereotypes, then, are crude mental pictures.

When somebody is prejudiced against something or a group of people they have a certain feeling or attitude toward them. As long as these feelings and attitudes remain inside as thoughts, no real damage can be done to anybody but ourselves. But as soon as these feelings are acted upon, we begin to **discriminate** against others. Here are three examples of discrimination.

- *'She's a New Age Traveller, so she doesn't deserve justice.'*
- *'He's black so he can't live here.'*
- *'She's a woman and so shouldn't be allowed to work here.'*

When early European explorers went to Africa, Australia and the Americas they did not understand the native peoples living there. They thought they were savages, and treated them dreadfully. For instance, within a few years of white Christian settlers stepping foot in Australia, 600 000 Aborigines died. The whites even hunted them as if they were animals. These dreadful things happen because ignorance *breeds* prejudice *which breeds* stereotyping *which breeds* discrimination *which breeds* destruction.

The world's religions

These prejudiced ways of seeing other human beings are condemned by all religions. All human beings are seen as being created equal. Nobody is superior to anyone else. We are all God's children. Here are some teachings from the world religions.

Bahá'í faith

'The earth is but one country and mankind its citizens.'

(Gleanings from the writings of Bahá'u'lláh)

Buddhism

'If we think of all the living beings as one body, one in wishing to be free from suffering, we will not hesitate to alleviate their suffering.'

(Geshe Kelsang)

Christianity

'From one man He created all races of mankind and made them live throughout the earth.'

(Acts 17: 26)

Islam

'All God's creatures are His family.'

(Hadith)

Judaism

'And if a stranger should live in your country, you must do him no wrong. The stranger who lives with you shall be as the home-born among you, and you shall love him like yourself.' (Leviticus 19: 33–34)

Sikhism

'Those who love God love everybody.'

(Guru Nanak)

Thousands of Aborigines were murdered by the white settlers in Australia

FOR DISCUSSION

'If I knew what my prejudices were I wouldn't have them.'

(W. H. Auden, English poet)

IN GROUPS

In groups of three or four try to work out some of the problems faced by:

a People from other cultures coming to live in Britain.

b Children being bullied at school because of the colour of their skin.

FOR YOUR FOLDERS

1 Explain these words: stereotype; scapegoats; prejudice; discriminate.

2 Explain how ignorance can lead to discrimination.

3 Make a list of some of the people in the world today who are discriminated against.

4 Explain why religions believe that prejudice and discrimination are wrong.

25 RACISM ●

In the last unit we looked at prejudice. One type of prejudice that has affected millions of people throughout the world, and still affects people today, is **racial discrimination** or **racism**. This means treating people differently because of their race or the colour of their skin.

The origins of racism

In Britain, racism developed in the eighteenth century, because some people wanted to become rich. The first merchants who started buying and selling slaves weren't doing so because they were necessarily prejudiced against Africans – they did it to make money. However, once society had accepted slavery it became very useful to think of black people as being inferior, as not being human. All the ignorant rumours about black people became a set of beliefs, and society accepted slavery.

The British rulers argued that only the white race could control the huge continents of Africa, India, the Americas and Australia. These beliefs led to the murder and the near extermination of whole tribes of Native American Indians in North and South America, the Aboriginal people in Tasmania and Australia, and the destruction of whole societies in Africa. Today, the terrible poverty that sweeps across many countries in Africa has its root cause in these early racist attitudes. Britain, and other European countries, became very rich by treating black people as less than human. While the rich got richer, the poor got poorer.

When Britain needed people to work after World War II the Government invited thousands of people over from India and the Caribbean. Yet as soon as there was no longer any need for their labour, and after they'd worked hard, people started calling for them to be 'sent home' (**repatriated**).

Racism in Britain always becomes more widespread during times of **recession** (when there is high unemployment). In some inner cities, for example, when jobs become scarce and money tight, black people become scapegoats (see Unit 24). This happens in some other European countries today. For instance, in Germany recently Turkish people have been treated as second-class citizens and some have been murdered by modern-day Nazis. Many people are worried about this, because of what happened to Jewish people in the 1930s and 1940s.

Example 1   The Holocaust

Racism can start from seemingly very small things, but it can lead to the most terrible things imaginable. In the 1930s the Nazis, under their leader, Adolf Hitler, began a programme to rid the world of all Jewish people. It was called 'The Final Solution' and the Nazis began to make Jewish people the scapegoat for all the problems facing Germany. By 1945, over six million Jews had died – most of them in the gas chambers of terrifying concentration camps. It is difficult for us to imagine the huge amount of human suffering involved.

Example 2   The Ku Klux Klan

In America millions of black slaves were treated as second class citizens. They were not allowed into certain public areas, and were separated from white people in such places as schools, restaurants and parks, because of the colour of their skin. It was not until 1965 that black people were allowed to vote. In the southern states of America, an organization known as the Ku Klux Klan terrorized black people. It burned black people's houses down, whipped them and killed them. The Ku Klux Klan wore white hoods and argued that God was white and all black people were inferior. The Ku Klux Klan still exists today.

Example 3   The British National Party

In Britain a movement known as the British National Party (BNP) exists, arguing that black people should be thrown out of this country (repatriated). The BNP is made up of people who are ignorant about black people and their cultures. Often members of the BNP are violent. Their arguments are unreliable because they fail to accept that:

- *Most black people were born in Britain and have parents and grandparents who were born here.*

- *Black people have contributed greatly to this country in many walks of life.*

The funeral of the victim of a racist attack in Britian

- *A country which has people from different cultures is a more exciting country and provides a greater variety of music, food, dress, religions, ideas and languages.*

- *Black people are not the **cause** of poverty and unemployment but the **victims**.*

Religious viewpoints

The world religions teach that all people are equal and should not be treated differently because of their race or colour. Many religious people throughout the world work towards ending racism. They believe that racism is:

- ***destructive** – it destroys people's lives*

- ***divisive** – it separates people from each other*

- ***dangerous** – it can lead to **genocide** (when one group deliberately sets out to destroy another group).*

Here is a quote about racism from the Bahá'í faith.

'God maketh no distinction between the white and the black ... God is no respecter of persons on account of either colour or race. All colours are acceptable unto Him, be they white, black or yellow.'

('Abdu'l-Bahá, in Advent of Divine Justice)

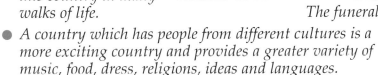

THINKING POINT
Political parties like the British National Party should be banned.

FOR YOUR FOLDERS

1 Explain the following words: holocaust, genocide, extermination, repatriated, recession, scapegoat, inferior.

2 Explain in your own words the origins of racism.

3 Write a paragraph on what you think the effects of racism can be.

4 Why do religious people think that racism is wrong?

FOR DISCUSSION

- *How do you think a child at school, who is the victim of a racist attack, can protect themself?*

- *There are an estimated 70 000 **racially motivated** attacks in England and Wales every year. How do you think society can prevent racist attitudes and protect victims of racially motivated attacks?*

26 ONE FOOT IN THE GRAVE? ••••••••

Ageism

'Old codger', 'Stupid old cow', 'Old fogey', 'Silly old man'.

How many times have you heard these terms? How many times have you used them, or expressions like them? How would you like to hear other people saying these things about you? The everyday use of terms like this is an example of **ageism**.

We are not born old. Perhaps because of this many of us see old people as being different from the rest of us.

KEY WORD
Ageism means discrimination against people because they are no longer young.

Stereotyping

To **stereotype** someone means to pigeon-hole them, or to have a fixed idea about them. The stereotypes that exist in our society about older people can be cruel and damaging.

FOR YOUR FOLDERS
Read through stereotypes 1–6 below, then try to match them with the statements marked A–F which disprove them.

1 All old people are 'dears' or 'miseries.'

2 Old age means poverty.

3 You can't teach an old dog new tricks.

4 Old people are unhealthy and need looking after.

5 Old people can't give anything to society.

6 Old people have one foot in the grave.

A Over 97% of people aged over 65 do not live in old people's homes. In a recent survey 78% of people over 55 described their health as good.

B Studies show that older people are just as able to learn as young people.

C Age doesn't change a person's personality.

D Michelangelo was 71 when he started work on St Peter's, Rome; Winston Churchill was 65 when he became Prime Minister.

E Across the world young people are just as likely to die as the old.

F People over 55 have 60% of the country's savings, and 40% own their own houses.

FOR DISCUSSION
Consequences
The consequences of stereotyping can seriously damage many people's chances of living happy lives. Read the following statements and discuss them.

- *Older people have the same feelings as the young, yet society expects them to be wise and good tempered, but dismisses them and treats them as fools at the same time.*

- *Most images of older people on television strengthen stereotypes.*

- *Old age should be a time of leisure and freedom, yet over half of elderly married couples live on less than £100 a week.*

- *Adverts are mostly about young people and seem to ignore the needs of older people.*

- *Older people are forced to retire even if they don't want to and people over 45 are highly unlikely to get jobs.*

TALKING POINTS
'Today's old are yesterday's providers and heroes.'

'Age is everybody's concern.'

'I didn't get the chance to stay on at school. I can't wait to retire and go back.'

'I know its been said before but if there's money for sending people to the moon, there should be enough for a decent old age pension.' (Age Concern, How will it feel to be old)

The view of some world religions

Judaism

'Listen to your father who gave you life, and do not despise your mother when she is old.'

(Proverbs 23: 22)

Islam

'Your Lord orders that you ... be kind to parents. If one or both of them attain old age with you, do not say one word of contempt to them, or repel them, but speak to them in terms of honour.'

(Qur'an 17: 23)

SILLY OLD MOO.

HOW LONG BEFORE PEOPLE CALL YOU NAMES? FIGHT AGEISM NOW. AGE

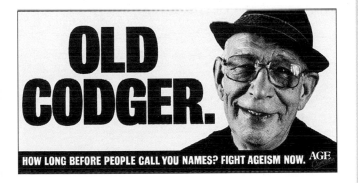

OLD CODGER.

HOW LONG BEFORE PEOPLE CALL YOU NAMES? FIGHT AGEISM NOW. AGE

*F*OR DISCUSSION

Somebody in the class should volunteer to read the following poem aloud. The poem was found in an old woman's locker in the hospital where she died.

What do you see nurses, what do you see?
Are you thinking when you are looking at me,
A crabbit old woman, not very wise,
Uncertain of habit, with faraway eyes,
Who dribbles her food and makes no reply,
when you say in a loud voice,
'I do wish you'd try.'
Who seems not to notice the things that you do
And forever is losing a stocking or shoe,
Who, unresisting or not, lets you do as you will,
With bathing and feeding the long day to fill,
Is that what you're thinking, is that what you see?
Then open your eyes nurse
You're not looking at me.
I'll tell you who I am as I sit here so still
As I use at your bidding, as I eat at your will,
I'm a small child of ten with a father and mother,
Brothers and sisters who love one another,
A young girl of sixteen with wings at her feet,
Dreaming that soon now a lover she'll meet,
A bride soon at twenty, my heart gives a leap,
Remembering the vows that I promised to keep,
At twenty-five now, I have young of my own,
Who need me to build a secure, happy home,
A young woman of thirty, my young now
      grow fast,
Bound to each other with ties that should last.
At forty my young ones, now grown, will
      soon be gone,
But my man stays beside me to see I don't mourn.
At fifty once more babies play round my knee,
Again we know children, my loved one and me.
Dark days are upon me, my husband is dead,
I look at the future, I shudder with dread.
For my young are all busy rearing young of
      their own,
I think of the years and the love I have known.
I'm an old woman now and nature is cruel,
'Tis her jest to make old age look like a fool,
The body it crumbles, grace and vigour depart,
There now is a stone where once I had a heart:
But inside this old carcass a young girl still dwells,
I remember the joys, I remember the pain,
And I'm loving and living life over again,
I think of the years all too few, gone too fast,
And accept the stark fact that nothing can last,
So open your eyes nurse, open and see,
Not a crabbit old woman,
Look closer, see ME...

27 VIOLENCE ● ● ● ● ● ● ● ● ● ● ● ● ● ● ● ● ● ●

Our television screens and newspaper headlines are full of violent images. It seems that we live in an increasingly violent world. Or do we? If we look back through history we find that it is often very violent. In the twentieth century, for instance, humankind has experienced violence on an enormous scale. Hitler's Nazis in Germany murdered over six million Jews as well as hundreds of thousands of other people such as gypsies, homosexuals and people with disabilities. On 6 August 1945, 140 000 people died when the Japanese city of Hiroshima was hit by an atomic bomb. Again, during World War II,

135 000 people died in just fourteen hours when Allied planes bombed the beautiful city of Dresden in Germany. Since then millions of people have died violently – and today wars destroy human lives right across this planet.

> **K**EY QUESTION
> *What makes people react violently?*

We all lose our tempers sometimes and many of us hit out at somebody, either with words or with fists. Most of us are capable of violence; most of us react violently when something goes wrong.

Quiz

THOU SHALT NOT KILL!
How violent are you?

1 Your younger brother spills coffee over your brand new shirt/blouse. Do you ...

   A *throttle him?*

   B *go mad and demand he pays for a new one?*

   C *accept that it was an accident?*

2 Someone at school calls you a reprobate. Do you ...

   A *lay into them?*

   B *call them a reprobate back?*

   C *ask them what a reprobate is?*

3 You're out in town and someone knocks into you. Do you ...

   A *threaten to rearrange their face?*

   B *tell them in no uncertain terms to be more careful?*

   C *ignore it – it was just an accident after all?*

4 You have an argument with your boy /girlfriend. They slap you across the face. Do you ...

   A *slap them back twice as hard?*

   B *say the most cruel and spiteful thing you can think of?*

   C *leave them alone to cool down?*

5 You've just spilt coffee over your homework which has taken all evening to finish. Do you ...

   A *kick the cat?*

   B *blame it on anyone who's around?*

   C *shrug your shoulders and accept that these things happen?*

6 You're out with your three year old sister. She runs out into the road and nearly gets run over. Do you ...

   A *smack her?*

   B *shake her to frighten her, so she doesn't do it again?*

   C *explain how dangerous it is?*

7 A cyclist nearly runs you down on the way home from school. Do you ...

   A *drag the cyclist off the bike and work him over?*

   B *tell him he's a delinquent and shouldn't be let loose even with a tricycle?*

   C *accept his apology?*

8 You're out with a group of friends when another group starts calling you a load of wallies. Do you ...

   A *kick hell out of them?*

   B *ignore them – but hope someone else kicks hell out of them?*

   C *ignore them?*

How did you score?

Mostly As:
Anyone who gets on the wrong side of you had better watch out. You fly off the handle easily and you don't mind who's in the way.

Mostly Bs:
You're not into inflicting GBH, but you don't mind giving someone a verbal earbashing if they deserve it.

Mostly Cs:
You keep your temper under control – but make sure you do stand up for yourself!

THINKING POINTS

'An eye for an eye and soon we shall all be blind.'

(Mahatma Gandhi – Indian leader who freed India from British rule without using violence)

'Violence is sexist. Historically, it has been done mostly by men.'

(New Internationalist)

GROUP WORK

In groups of ten discuss the following:

1. 'throttle him', 'lay into him', 'threaten to rearrange their faces', 'work him over', 'kick the hell out of them'
   This is murderous language. If you answered 'A' to the questions in the quiz, do you think you might be capable of murder?

2. Can you think of any circumstances when you think it is acceptable to kill a fellow human being?

3. In what ways can we turn our anger into positive and creative pastimes?

Reflection

Wendy and Tim Parry, the parents of Tim Parry, aged twelve, who was killed by an IRA bomb in Warrington, said, 'You walk into his bedroom and see a bed that has not been slept in. You see his clothes and possessions lying unused. That is when it tears at your heart.'

All the world religions teach that it is wrong to harm another human being. Sadly, over the centuries, many people have killed others – sometimes because they were from a different religion. Sometimes they have argued that under certain circumstances it is acceptable to kill another human being. However, the sacred scriptures of all the world religions say, that under most circumstances, it is wrong to kill.

They all agree that violence is:

wasteful – it uproots and destroys precious human lives and it destroys human intelligence

unsafe – it is hard to limit its deadly effects to those who are guilty

unjust – innocent people lose their lives and families are ripped apart

destructive – it treats people like objects and makes people brutal

blind – it fails to see that human life is a wonderful gift.

THINKING POINT

'To begin with, of course, we must control the anger and hatred in ourselves. As we learn to remain in peace, then we can demonstrate in society in a way that makes a real statement for world peace. If we ourselves remain always angry and then sing about world peace, it has little meaning.' (The Dalai Lama – spiritual leader of the Tibetan Buddhists)

THINGS TO DO

Read the following newspaper report. Conduct a survey to find out what the people in your class think.

TOO MUCH TV VIOLENCE

Viewers believe there is a link between real life and television violence, according to the results of a survey published today. They think there is too much violence on TV and the 9.30 p.m. watershed is too early. The *TV Times* survey shows 59% felt that there were links between television and real life violence. Another 85% said TV companies were not being careful enough in their monitoring of screen violence. Overall 52% said there was too much violence. Male and female views differed, with 38% of men saying there was too much violence as against 63% of women. But of viewers under eighteen only 15% felt there was too much TV violence and 84% said they found violent films acceptable on screen.

28 BULLYING ••••••••••••••••••••••••••••

Every so often a tragedy occurs and somebody who has been bullied commits suicide. Bullying occurs every day in schools around the country. Children's lives are made a misery. Bullies can be both boys and girls.

There are many important questions that need to be answered about bullying. In this section you will be encouraged to think about bullying and discuss it with your classmates.

KEY IDEAS
- *A bully might be a very unhappy person, angry with their own life and taking this anger out on others.*
- *The bully is the person with real, long lasting problems.*

KEY QUESTION 1
Why do people become bullies?

FOR DISCUSSION
There are many possible reasons why some children become bullies. Discuss these ideas with your classmates:

- *Bullies have been bullied themselves.*
- *Bullies don't think much of themselves. Often they dislike themselves and so they find somebody to pick on.*
- *By picking on somebody weaker than themselves, bullies feel better about themselves for a while.*
- *Through bullying, a 'pecking order' is set up in the school, class or group.*

KEY QUESTION 2
What does it mean to feel happy about yourself and to be in control of your life?

Factfile
Bullies may pick on somebody they see as **pathetic** – somebody who already seems unhappy or downtrodden. This is what is meant by an **easy target**. This **victim** may remind the bully, who is already unhappy, of themselves.

- *Bullies like to think they are 'big' by bullying somebody behind the teacher's back.*
- *Bullies want to be boss. By bullying others they feel they are in control of their own lives. Often a bully will pick on somebody they think has control of their own life (for instance, someone who is perhaps doing well at school, or comes from a happy family, or is 'better off').*
- *The bully might be jealous of the victim's life (for example, the victim may be admired by other people for something).*
- *The bully might be angry with his or her life and takes this anger out on somebody else.*

ARE COWARDS

ARE VICTIMS

WANT TO BE NUMBER ONE

ARE UNHAPPY ABOUT THEMSELVES

Bullies ...

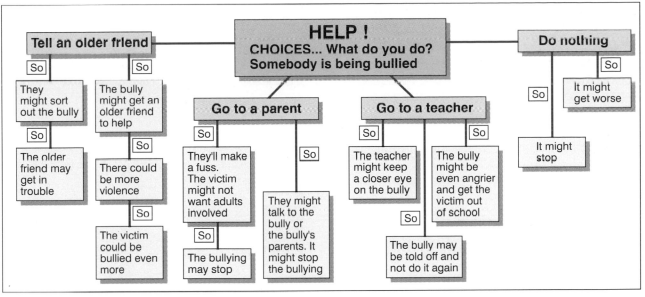

Choices – what do you do?

KEY QUESTIONS 3

What should you do if you saw somebody bullying or if you were the victim of bullying?

- *If you saw bullying going on, would you report it?*
- *If you answered 'yes', explain why you would.*
- *If you answered 'no', explain why you wouldn't.*
- *Bullies usually have back-up – others who hang around with them. Why do you think bullies' 'friends' hang around with them?*
- *Would you hang around with a bully?*
- *It not, why not? What if the bully is a friend of yours who has only recently turned to bullying?*
- *Would you report your friend if you saw that he or she was hurting the victim, and making his or her life a misery?*

KEY QUESTION 4

Why are victims of bullying often afraid or unwilling to tell others about it?

KEY IDEA

The bully is the person with the real problem.

THINGS TO DO

This unit gives only a brief summary of the choices open to you about bullying. Discuss them in pairs or groups of three and then write down some of the problems that these choices might create.

THINKING POINTS

'You have heard that it was said, "Love your friends, hate your enemies". But now I tell you, love your enemies and pray for those who persecute you, so that you may become the sons of your Father in heaven. For He makes His sun to shine on bad and good people alike ....'

(*Jesus, in Matthew 5: 43–5*)

'Do for others what you want them to do for you.'

(*Jesus, in Matthew 7: 12*)

29 JUST A GAME?

Over one and a half million homes in Britain have Nintendo and Sega video games, and millions more have other makes of computer games. Some teachers, doctors and scientists are worried about what these games might be doing to young people's minds. Even the makers of Nintendo and Sega are now putting health warnings on the games following an outbreak of epilepsy among young players.

A survey conducted in Manchester found that almost half the children showed signs of **addiction** to video games. An addiction means somebody can't stop themselves following their habit. These young people, aged between thirteen and fifteen, were playing video games for up to 25 hours every week.

The video game industry is worth about £9 billion worldwide. The games are expensive. Children from poor homes can't afford them and each year some products go quickly out of date, and so children put pressure on parents to buy new ones.

QUESTIONNAIRE

Are you addicted to video games?
If you answer 'yes' to more than four questions, then you may be addicted.
Do you:

- *play most days*
- *often play for long periods*
- *play for excitement*
- *get restless if you don't play*
- *play for a personal best*
- *often try to limit playing*
- *play instead of doing your homework*
- *stop meeting with your friends and talking with them?*

If you answered 'yes' to any of these questions, what effects do you think computer games have on your life and the lives of your friends?

Special effects?

Just a game?

Some scientists and teachers believe that video games:

- *stop young people from talking to each other*
- *stop young children from reading and writing*
- *make young people more **aggressive***
- *can cause **photosensitive epilepsy** which is set off by the flashing light effect of the games*
- *are **sexist** – women are shown as being helpless victims*
- *are **racist** – often foreigners are seen as being 'the baddies'*
- *are **stressful**.*

Reflections

'Some of the games show you violent moves which you can later practise on your friends. Some of my friends start fighting and think they are in a video game.'

(Nicholas, aged eleven)

'They are just games and they are exciting. I don't think anyone believes that they are true. I like to play them because they're better than watching television.'

(Jaspar, aged thirteen)

'Playing these games can lead to anti-social behaviour, make children aggressive and affect their emotional stability.'

(Professor Cary Cooper, University of Manchester)

'The games not only help children to use computers but also set them difficult tasks. They have to find the solutions and this is what life is about.'

(Simon Morris, Marketing Director of Sega UK)

THINGS TO DO

Read the following advertisement. Carefully try to pick out some of the violent words used to sell the product, e.g.'psychos'.

▲ Splatterhouse III: 16 megs of action!

Just as you're getting over the rampant nausea brought on by the prequel, the third in Namco's Splatterhouse series is all set to puke onto your Megadrive.

Splatterhouse 3 continues the bloodthirsty brawling horror in a similar vein (pardon the pun) this time pitting Rick the 'Rough and Ready' against legions of gruesome fiends out for blood, his in particular, in a desperate attempt to save his family.

The 16-meg game apparently features level after level of chillingly horrendous graphics, multiple endings, nonlinear gameplay, wicked new levels and all in all sounds totally one for the sickos and psychos (or people after a good beat 'em up for that matter).

Just a game?

1 How many violent words can you find?

2 When the advertisement refers to the 'sickos and psychos', who is it referring to, the monster, the 'hero' or the player?

Viewpoints

'The best people to deal with the problem in the first place are parents. We should like to see parents control the amount of time their children spend on computer games.'

(Jackie Miller, Teacher)

'We live in a mysterious universe, and there are so many questions that remain unanswered. There is so much suffering in the world that could be prevented. Why do we train children to sit in front of a tiny screen blowing people up – like little gods? Surely, it would be better if they were taught to think about and help the less fortunate, the poor and the sick in the world.' (Author's interview)

THINKING POINTS

'All that we are is the result of what we have thought.'

(Buddhist teaching, Dhammapada, 1)

'What he thinks is what he really is.'

(Proverbs 23: 7)

'Riches do not come from an abundance of goods but from a contented mind.'

(Muhammad, in the Hadith, 69)

KEY QUESTIONS

● *Do you think violent video games increase your feelings of fear about the world?*

● *Do they make you feel better about the world, or do they make you aggressive, stressed, bad-tempered or anti-social?*

● *How do these games represent 'heroes', women and people from other countries?*

● *Are they about good and evil? Can they be evil themselves?*

30 THE GREAT DIVIDE ●●●●●●●●●●●●●●

We live in a world in which there is a great divide. While some people live in absolute luxury, others die in absolute poverty. This great divide can be found today in Britain.

> ### KEY QUESTIONS
> - *Does money make you happy?*
> - *Does money make somebody a better person?*
> - *Is it right that one person can own so much, and so many own so little?*
> - *How much is a person worth?*

The richest people in Britain
How much are they worth?

The top ten

Gad and Hans Reusing	food packers	£4000 million
David Sainsbury and family	grocers	£3400 million
Garfield Weston	food producer	£2110 million
John and Adrian Swire	shipping and airlines	£2000 million
John Paul Getty	oil	£1600 million
The Duke of Westminster	landowner	£1500 million
Sri and Gopi Hinduja	financiers	£1350 million
Sir John Moores and family	football pools	£1350 million
Charles Feeney	duty free shopping	£850 million
George Soros	financier	£750 million

Among the other richest people in Britain are:

Richard Branson	airlines	£475 million
Paul McCartney	pop music	£450 million
Paul Raymond	pornography and property	£200 million
Elton John	pop music	£120 million
Anita Roddick	The Body Shop	£100 million
Mick Jagger	pop music	£90 million
Earl Spencer and family	landowner	£84 million
George Michael	pop music	£80 million
John Menzies	newsagent	£75 million
Mark Knopfler	pop music	£60 million

How much is

£10
£100
£1000
£10 000
£100 000
a million? £1 000 000
and a billion? £1 000 000 000

FOR DISCUSSION
'As long as there is poverty in the world I can never be rich, even if I have a million dollars. I can never be what I ought to be until you are what you ought to be.'

(Dr Martin Luther King)

THINKING POINT
'But those who want to get rich fall into temptation and are caught in the trap of many foolish and harmful desires, which pull them down to ruin and destruction. For the love of money is a source of all kinds of evil.'

(1 Timothy 6: 9, 10)

The poorest people in Britain

Millions of people today live below the so-called **poverty line**. This means they barely have enough to live on. They live in bad housing, in areas of high crime and with little or no money for their bills. More and more people are becoming homeless (see Unit 31). Often we might see these people in our towns and cities. We know nothing about their lives yet each one of them has their own story. They have no wealth. While the rich own huge houses these people live on the streets.

IN PAIRS

You have just won £1 million on the pools. A new law says you can live off £100 000 but you must give the rest away to help the poor. Discuss which poor people and organizations you'd give the money to. Give reasons for your choices.

IN PAIRS – *the two Johns*

In pairs, look at the two photographs below. Imagine you are each a different one of the Johns. Write a diary of a normal day in the life of the John you have chosen to be. After you've both written your diaries, compare notes.

TALKING POINTS

'As Jesus was starting on his way again, a man ran up, knelt before him, and asked him, "Good Teacher, what must I do to receive eternal life?" ... Jesus looked straight at him with love and said, "You need only one thing! Go and sell all you have and give the money to the poor, and you will have riches in heaven; and then come and follow me."'

(Mark 10: 17–21)

'It is much harder for a rich person to enter the Kingdom of God than for a camel to go through the eye of a needle.'

(Mark 10: 25)

The five richest people in the world

1	Sultan of Brunei	oil	$37 billion (£19 billion)
2	Walton family	retailing	$24 billion (£12.5 billion)
3	Mars family	confectionery	$13 billion (£6.75 billion)
4	Newhouse brothers	publishing	$13 billion (£6.75 billion)
5	Queen Elizabeth II		$11.7 billion (£6 billion)

The family fortune of Sir John Swire is £2000 million

John, homeless, living around Leicester Square: 'I was in the Special Boat Service. I went to fight in the Falklands with my two brothers. They were both killed there. After I came home, my daughter died from an overdose of heroin. I started drinking and found myself on the streets.'

31 ON THE STREETS •••••••••••••••••

This section looks at a growing problem that faces many young people living on the streets in Britain.

Street children in Britain

Sometimes when the pressures get too great, the only way out seems to be to get away from it all. It is estimated that about 98 000 young people go missing each year in Britain. Most are aged between fourteen and sixteen. There are many reasons why these young people decide to leave home. Here are just a few.

- *Problems at home: not getting on with parents or step-parents; violence; sexual abuse*
- *Problems in care: bullying; being fed up with being in care; not being involved in decisions about their future*
- *Problems at school: being suspended and afraid to face parents*

Task 1

Imagine you have run away. It is your first night in a strange city. You have no money. Write down some of the thoughts that might be going through your head and some of the feelings you'd be having. Then write down some of the dangers that could face you.

The generation gap

Sometimes you might find it difficult to talk to older people, particularly your parents. This is sometimes called an **intergenerational communication** problem.

Group work

In small groups, discuss ways of trying to improve intergenerational communication. Here are some questions to help you.

1 If you feel intergenerational communication in your family is not all it could be, what would you say are the causes?

2 If you feel intergenerational communication in your family is poor, what effects do you think this has had upon you, and upon the rest of your family?

3 If you feel that intergenerational communication in your family cannot be improved, what reasons can you give for feeling this way?

4 If you believe intergenerational communication in your family can be improved what suggestions do you have for bringing this about?

5 If there is a breakdown in communication in a group, do you think that the members of that group could search for things they have in common?

6 If members of a group have different interests, does that rule out their communicating with one another?

7 Is it possible that members of different generations have had very similar experiences?

Many young people leaving home end up on the streets

On the streets

They say I'm a street kid,
but how easily they forget,
who I am and how
I ended up like this.

They say I'm violent,
but I tell you that
poverty is violent and
it gives me no choice.

They say I am bad,
but if I steal what I can,
it's because they hold the keys
to the riches of life.

They say I'm past all hope,
but it was they who put me here
when they stole my parents' land
and left them hunger wages.

They say I'm rough and dirty,
but if I search through rubbish dumps
it's because their precious ones
are dressed up like princes.

They say my parents are to blame,
but the rich folk showed no scruples
when they threw my family off the land
and abandoned them to the street.

(Christian Aid)

The Children's Society

The Children's Society is a charity that helps children living in poverty and without homes. The Society has 132 projects throughout England and Wales, all working for children and young people. These include family centres where young families with problems can meet, residential units which offer help for children with special problems in their lives, ordinary housing where young people with disabilities can live in the community, home-finding, which finds loving homes for children with disabilities, and safe houses where young runaways on the street can find refuge.

The Children's Society is a Christian organization which believes that as well as looking at the effects of homelessness, our society must do something about the causes of homelessness.

TASK 2

Read the following piece about a safe house. In a group, discuss why safe houses are important for homeless children.

Leeds safe house

Alex was a terrified nine year old, cold and alone and facing dangers every night on the streets of London's busy West End. 'You don't have time to feel anything – you get caught up just trying to survive,' said Alex, now seventeen but a runaway again – this time from unhappiness and abuse in a children's home. The difference now is that she has found refuge in Leeds Safe House, opened by the Children's Society's North East Region in 1991.

'I have been on the streets on and off since I was nine years old. The Safe House is the place where I got my first hug,' said Alex. 'In Safe Houses you know you are going to be listened to. When I was five, I told a schoolteacher what was happening. She told me not to make up dirty stories. So I kept my mouth shut.'

(The Children's Society)

FOR YOUR FOLDERS

Life on the streets is very tough – cold nights, child prostitution, drug dealers, drunks, violence. You have no money, little food and no place to go. You wander aimlessly every day. There's nobody to care for you and love you when you're ill. Imagine you are on the streets. Write a diary entry describing, 'A week in the life of …'.

32 CRIME ••••••••••••••••••••••••••••••••••••••

Somebody commits a crime when they break a law. There are many reasons why people break the law and commit a crime. Some of them include:

Social pressures
We live in a materialistic society in which we are encouraged to have lots of possessions. Television and advertising are full of images about what life should be like, but these images are very different from the reality of life for most people.

Circumstances
People who commit crimes are more likely to come from areas of high unemployment and bad housing, and are likely to have had a deprived upbringing.

Personal problems
Some people have very unhappy childhoods – violence at home, broken marriages, difficult parents. These can lead to some young people expressing their anger and frustration through crime.

Lack of community
Some people who are trapped in high-rise flats or huge sprawling council estates, with no sense of belonging, commit crime because they don't feel they are part of any community.

One of the main causes of crime is bad housing and the huge gap between rich and poor

Space
Poor people live in cramped conditions whereas well-off people have larger houses, gardens and uncrowded neighbourhoods. Lack of space can create tension, arguments, violence, frustration and crime.

Lack of self-esteem
In the New Testament, Jesus, quoting his Jewish Bible, taught, *'Love your neighbour as you love yourself,' (Matthew 22: 39)*. First, this means that we should try to treat other people the way we'd like to be treated, and second we'll never be able to love other people until we learn to love ourselves. But what does it mean to love yourself?

Self-love is
- *being kind to yourself*
- *trying to understand why you do things*
- *allowing yourself to make mistakes because it's only through making mistakes that you learn what is right and wrong.*

Self-love isn't
- *showing off*
- *bragging*
- *thinking you are the most important person in the world and not thinking about how other people feel.*

Of course, greed also makes people commit crimes. And many people who have to cope with the difficulties above still don't commit crimes. Why do you think they don't?

Why do some young people commit crime?
Here are some possible answers. On television, and in adverts and magazines, young people are encouraged to spend, spend, spend. They are told there is a certain way to look, a certain way to impress others. There is a lot of pressure on young people to behave in a certain way – these

pressures force some young people into crime.

Many people have very little money. Yet they live in a society which says money is important. If you've got no money and no prospects of a job or future, then crime might seem an attractive alternative.

For some people, life seems boring and meaningless. They commit crime because it brings adventure and risk into their lives and makes them feel that they've got a purpose. They reach a stage where they don't care if they get caught – anything is better than a boring existence.

For some young people a life of crime makes them feel important. They feel different from other people – it makes them feel big. If a person belongs to a group or a gang, they may feel that being involved in crime will gain them respect in the group.

Vox Pop

'In our society we are all encouraged to want things ... personal stereos, computer games, videos, CDs, big houses, fancy cars, exotic holidays, nice clothes, the latest gear. Yet, this same society is organized in such a way that millions of people are unable to get work or are in very low paid jobs. We are taught to be greedy and unhappy if we haven't got all these things, which we'll never have anyway.'

(Amanda, aged sixteen)

'The causes of crime are very deep. Some young people can't find a reason for living. Happiness in our society means having lots of money and impressing others. Yet true happiness doesn't come from what we have or what we pretend to be – it comes from helping other people around us, giving people our friendship and sharing the things we have.'

(Richard, aged seventeen)

'Our country spends billions of pounds on nuclear weapons. If this money was spent on improving other people's lives, especially in the slums and inner cities, people wouldn't have to turn to crime.' (John, aged fourteen)

Why do you think more and more people are turning to a life of crime?

It's simple – while the rich get richer, the poor get poorer. This is the cause of crime.'

(Alan, aged thirteen)

FOR YOUR FOLDERS

How does it feel to be a **victim** of crime? People who commit crimes don't often ask themselves this question. Write down how the following people and their families might feel.

1 A 78 year old woman is walking home to her flat. Two thirteen year old boys push her to the ground, grab her handbag and kick her in the face.

2 An Indian boy walking home from school is attacked by three youths. They beat him up and call him names. He staggers home covered in blood.

3 John's mum has saved up all year to buy him a mountain bike for Christmas. Although John always locks it, he returns from the supermarket to find it gone.

4 If those who commit crime and those who run the country applied the Golden Rule (*'Do for others what you want them to do for you.'*) to the way our society works, crime might be reduced. What do you think?

33 JOYRIDING OR DEATHRIDING? ••••

People taking vehicles without the permission of the owners and then driving them away has become a serious problem in parts of Britain. Although the offence is known as **joyriding**, some people call it **deathriding**.

Britain has the worst record in the world for joyriding. Nearly 40% of car crime offences are committed by young people (**juveniles**) under the age of seventeen. Most joyriders are young and are almost always male.

Studies show that most joyriders start taking and driving cars between the ages of thirteen and fifteen. Many become involved, as passengers at first, when they are much younger – some as young as ten.

The risks are enormous. In West Yorkshire, one in every nine **fatal** road crashes (when people are killed) involves a stolen car. Stolen vehicles are frequently speeding, and are twice as likely to go into a skid. They can cause:

- *death or injury to driver*
- *death or injury to passengers*
- *death or injury to innocent bystanders.*

The Law

The punishment for joyriding carries a maximum sentence of two years in jail, or five years if a death is involved. There is also an automatic driving ban and an unlimited fine. Drivers and passengers are held equally responsible.

However, many offenders are too young to be affected by the new law. Those under fourteen cannot be sentenced by a court to be held in a young offenders' institution. The maximum sentence for fourteen and fifteen year olds is one year and for sixteen to eighteen year olds, it is two years.

Why do they do it?

Here are some reasons. Can you think of any others?

- *Joyriding is exciting and is attractive to young people who feel that life is boring.*
- *Joyriding gives young people a feeling of power.*
- *Joyriding gives people a great thrill or 'buzz'.*
- *Powerful advertising for high powered cars, and glamorous images of high speed car chases in films, make young people worship them.*
- *Sometimes people take parts from the car before it is dumped.*
- *Some young people enjoy taunting the police and racing against them.*

THINKING POINTS

'We have trained a whole generation of young men to worship the motor car and to seek an identity through them. Films like **Terminator 2** and **Mad Max** glorify high speed car chases, but rarely show the gore that results in real life.'

(Dr Roy Light, expert on car crime)

'Do not bow down to any idol or worship it.'

(Exodus 20: 5)

FOR DISCUSSION

- *Why do some young people go joyriding?*
- *What are the dangers of joyriding?*
- *Do you think advertising makes people worship things?*
- *Do you think that some young people have 'lost meaning in their lives'?*
- *What do you think helps us to find 'meaning in life'?*

FOR YOUR FOLDERS

Read the two articles 'A joyrider speaks' and 'Deadly consequences'. Discuss

- *Why do you think Stuart was tempted to become a joyrider?*
- *What are the deadly consequences of joyriding?*
- *What sentences do you think joyriders should receive in the courts?*

The car before the joyriders stole it...

...and after

A JOYRIDER SPEAKS

Stuart was fourteen when he first had the urge to jump into a car – anyone's car – and drive it away. 'I'd got a Saturday job in a scrapyard, and I used to muck about in the old bangers,' he said. 'Then I started breaking into cars and driving them away with my mates. I used to watch my dad driving. I'd watch his feet really closely. It was easy to learn.'

Like most joyriders, Stuart fancied himself as an expert driver and a match for the police. But although he is now in his mid-twenties, he still does not have a licence. He remains disqualified because of his long list of motor-related convictions.

'First I got caught for under-age driving. Then I had an accident – not a bad one – and got cautioned. When I was seventeen I was sent to a young offenders' centre for four months. I gave it up for a while and even got a job. But I've always been car mad. I've had loads of sentences for car crimes – theft, unauthorised taking, you name it. None of them put me off.'

Stuart describes his family background in Derby as a happy one. But he hated school and hated working for £25 a week on a training scheme.

'I lost interest. I wanted to be out with the lads. I spent my sixteenth birthday driving down the motorway at 130 mph, with nine of us in a stolen car egging each other on. It's difficult to describe the feeling you get. I suppose it's about being in control of that much power. We used to get a real kick out of giving the Old Bill a chase. You didn't think about the risks to yourself or anyone else.'

(Guardian)

DEADLY CONSEQUENCES

It is just over a year since Carol Whittingham's 27 year old son Steven was killed in a collision with joyriders.

'It was around 7.20 p.m. We think Steven had just popped out to put some petrol in the car. He'd even left the TV and fire on.'

The crash happened just 20 metres from his home, in Brighouse, West Yorkshire. 'A car came down the hill on the wrong side of the road at an estimated speed of 80 mph. It hit Steven's car head-on. He didn't have a chance. The car thieves' vehicle ended up in a playground where it burst into flames, trapping them inside.'

The joyriders escaped thanks to a friend of Steven's who ran out of his nearby shop with a fire extinguisher. 'They got out and legged it, leaving my son for dead. Steven's friend only realised later what had happened. He's a nervous wreck as a result.'

She adds: 'It was an eighteen year old driving the stolen car, with a thirteen year old on board. They caught them later. We think it was when the driver showed up for treatment at the hospital to which my son was taken. The eighteen year old came up for trial at Leeds Crown Court. He's got two previous convictions for joyriding, and pleaded guilty. All he got was three years' youth custody, which means he'll be out in a few months' time. The younger one is a habitual car thief, but he'll not go before the courts, of course.'

For Carol Whittingham, her husband and their three surviving children, the trial was a travesty. 'They should call it "deathriding", not "joyriding". We end up serving the life sentence. In court they didn't even make a reference to what we're suffering.'

She says that she now suffers from phobias, such as not being able to close the bedroom door because she was in bed when the crash happened. 'Yet despite all this you have to carry on.'

(Guardian)

34 PUNISHMENT •••••••••••••••••••••••

The aims of punishment

When somebody is arrested for committing a crime they are punished. There are five main aims of punishment:

- *To protect society from somebody's anti-social behaviour.*
- *To put other people off from committing the same crime. (This is called deterrence.)*
- *To punish an offender with a punishment that fits the crime.*
- *To make the offender a better person so they don't commit further crimes. (This is called* **reform***.)*
- *To help society run smoothly and make people respect the law.*

THINKING POINTS

'Whichever one of you has committed no sin may throw the first stone ....'

(Jesus, in John 8: 7)

' ... never pay back evil for evil.'

Letter of Paul to the Romans (12: 17, New Testament)

'A person will reap exactly what he sows.'

Letter of Paul to the Galatians (6: 7, New Testament)

CLASS DEBATE

The ultimate punishment

The ultimate punishment is **capital punishment** or the **death sentence**. Although this form of punishment is no longer used in Britain, it is still carried out in many parts of the world.

After reading the following arguments, organize a class debate, *'This house believes that capital punishment is evil'*.

The case for capital punishment

- *Terrorists who kill innocent people should be hanged.*
- *It deters (puts off) potential murderers.*
- *It has been in existence since the beginning of time, so why abolish it now?*
- *It protects civilians and police.*
- *It expresses society's horror of murder.*
- *A so-called life sentence is not punishment enough.*
- *Some 'lifers' are back on the streets in a few years.*
- *The law should punish the crime of murder with murder.*
- *Revenge is a natural human emotion.*
- *Capital punishment helps the victim's family to get over their loss.*

The case against capital punishment

- *Capital punishment may make convicted terrorists into martyrs.*
- *The law condemns murder and then goes on to murder in the name of the law.*
- *It does not necessarily stop murders.*
- *The death penalty is cruel.*
- *Society turns the executioner into a murderer.*
- *In the past the wrong person has been hanged.*
- *It makes a mockery of the idea of reform.*
- *Rather than kill so-called murderers we should begin to study their motives and the pressures society has put them under.*
- *All life is sacred – what right has society to judge that a person's life should end?*
- *Sometimes the electric chair or hanging does not work and the victim is in great pain. This is unfair to members of the family.*

A Humanist viewpoint

'Capital punishment has been the concern of humanists for years. Revenge, whether divine or human, is always destructive, never creative. It has no place in any society claiming to be civilized.'

(Kit Mouat, What Humanism Is About)

*F*OR DISCUSSION – **You're the judge**

It looks like a clear case of theft. A teenager has been caught stealing a mountain bike. If you were the judge what sentence would you pass? Think about the different aims of punishment.

The story

John is sixteen. He's been caught red-handed, by a local policeman, stealing a mountain bike. He's been charged and is appearing in court. It's his first offence.

John

'I'm unemployed. I don't get any dole money and I don't want to go on Youth Training. My parents haven't got work. If I had a job I wouldn't have stolen the bike.'

The police

'This young man hasn't been in trouble with us before. However, we have to punish him now in case he turns to more serious crime.'

John's father

'We're a poor family. I wish I could afford to buy John things but I can't. If there were more decent jobs there'd be less crime. John's a good lad – he helps around the house and has never been in any trouble. I blame the way our society is always encouraging young people to want more – it makes them unhappy when they can't afford these things.'

Prosecutor

'This is a case of theft. The law is clear. Such offences should be punished. Although it's his first offence the court must make an example of him so that others will be put off from stealing.'

The victim

What do you think the person who had their bike stolen might say?

Possible sentences

A fine

The amount will be based on how serious the crime is and how much John can afford.

Detention

In a young offenders' institution, the minimum length of stay is two months, up to a maximum of twelve months.

Probation

John is 'let off' but is warned about his future conduct. If he is convicted of another offence, he can be sentenced for this one too.

Supervision order

John would be supervised, that is be instructed to live in one place for a certain period of time so the police could keep an eye on him.

Community service

John would work in the community to repay the community for his crime.

Curfew

John would have to spend certain hours of the day at home. To ensure he does this, the courts could use an **electronic monitoring system**, although they are unlikely to impose this sentence on a first time offender.

Courts can combine probation, supervision and community service if they feel this is appropriate. John could also be acquitted if the judge found him not guilty or there wasn't enough evidence against him.

35 MAKING LOVE ••••••••••••••••••

Most healthy human beings are able to reproduce. Unlike some less complicated forms of life, we do this **sexually** involving the male and female of our species.

The sexual drive is one of the most powerful drives known to physically mature human beings. However, human beings are different from most other animals because our sex drive is linked to our feelings. This means that when human beings have sex, how they feel about each other is very important.

Sex is something that sooner or later we all have to think about. The consequences of sexual activity are very important. Here are some things that people who have sex have to think about very seriously.

KEY QUESTIONS 1

- *How do I feel about my partner?*
- *Do I like them just because I want to enjoy their body?*
- *Do I love them? What does it mean to love somebody?*
- *Will I stay with this person?*
- *Can this person trust me? Am I worthy of their trust?* ➤

- *Do I respect them as a person?*
- *What do I know about this person?*

Making love with another person brings tremendous responsibilities. Although people often use contraceptives (see Unit 36) to prevent pregnancy, the risk of pregnancy is always there.

KEY QUESTIONS 2

These are some questions couples need to ask.

- *What are the possibilities of me getting AIDS or another sexually transmitted disease?*
- *Am I prepared to become pregnant?*
- *Am I prepared to become a father?*
- *Do I love this person enough to stay with them, even if we have a child?*

IN PAIRS

Discuss with a friend Key Questions 1 and 2. Write down some of your ideas in your folder.

Relationships bring many responsibilities

FOR YOUR FOLDERS

Read these two letters. What advice would you give to the young people who wrote them?

1 I am thirteen and have a boyfriend who is nearly sixteen. He keeps putting pressure on me to have sex, saying that it's natural for girls of my age. I don't want to have sex yet, but I don't want to lose him. What should I do?

2 I am fourteen and my voice is breaking and I'm growing pubic hair. I've not really been interested in girls before. But now, because all my mates have girlfriends, I feel I ought to as well. But I know it's not really what I want to do – I'd prefer to be playing football. But some kids get called names if they don't have a girlfriend. What should I do?

Religious views on making love

Buddhism

'... Certain actions cause suffering and are therefore to be avoided.'

(Rev Daishia Morgan, The Place of Sexuality in Training)

Christianity

'But in the beginning at the time of creation, "God made them male and female", as the scripture says. And for this reason a man will leave his father and mother and unite with his wife, and the two will become one.'

(Jesus, in Mark 10: 6–8)

Islam

'When a husband and wife share intimacy it is rewarded and a blessing from Allah.' (Hadith)

Sikhism

'Real union between husband and wife occurs when the heart of one dies in the other's and they become one as a necklace of pearls with the passing of a thread through them.'

(Guru Granth Sahib)

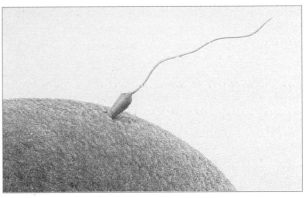

The moment of conception

IN GROUPS

In small groups of about three or four, discuss the following.

● Why do people often make jokes about sex?

● Why do some people feel embarrassed when the topic of sex comes up?

● What sort of ideas about sex do we get from television, newspapers and magazines? Are these ideas always truthful?

● Imagine you had to plan a sex education programme for people of your own age. There are ten sessions of 45 minutes to organize. What topics would you like to cover? Take twenty minutes to do this. Then write down on a piece of paper your suggestions and fold the paper, before handing it to the teacher, who will arrange a class discussion.

● What do you think the quotes from the world religions mean?

36 CONTRACEPTION ● ● ● ● ● ● ● ● ● ● ● ● ● ● ●

More teenage girls than ever are becoming mothers. In the UK the number of pregnancies amongst fourteen year old girls nearly doubled between 1979 and 1989. In many schools with more than 1000 pupils, up to six girls every year are becoming pregnant.

FOR DISCUSSION

- *Many girls are unwilling to talk about contraception with their boyfriends.*
- *Experts say more classroom discussion should be about relationships and contraception.*
- *In a recent survey 66% of pupils aged thirteen and fourteen said they'd received very little information on contraception.*
- *Boys and girls need to know more about how each other feel about sex and love.*

KEY WORD

Contraception – Various methods a couple can use to avoid an unwanted pregnancy.

Methods of contraception

Natural Family Planning (NFP)

NFP means the woman becoming aware of her own fertile and infertile cycles by recording the natural signals of her body. Many Roman Catholics prefer these methods.

Does it work?

The World Health Organization puts the **sympothermal** method in the top three methods of birth control.

Rhythm method

Some days during the menstrual cycle a woman is not fertile – so a couple can have sex during those days. But they need to work out the 'safe' days very carefully indeed. The woman will have to take her temperature regularly – and this has to be done every month as the cycle is different every time.

Does it work?

This method is not 'safe' at all, as it is so easy to make a mistake.

Withdrawal method

The man withdraws his penis before his sperm are released, so that none of them enters the woman's vagina.

Does it work?

No, because the man may not withdraw his penis in time. Also, sperm can be released at any time while the couple are having sex.

The Pill

The Pill is now taken by about 55 million women worldwide. It works by altering the hormone balance of the woman's body so that she does not become fertile.

Does it work?

As a method of contraception, it is the safest. There may be side-effects in that other parts of the body such as the breasts or body hair may be affected. Women taking the Pill may also suffer from depression. The long-term effects are not known.

The vault cap and the diaphragm

These are both rubber domes on a flexible ring. The diaphragm is wider and flatter. Both are smeared with contraceptive jelly and slipped into the woman's vagina. The cap fits over the mouth of the cervix. The diaphragm fits right across the vagina. Both must be fitted by a doctor and checked regularly or they will not work. They must be left in place for at least six hours after the couple have had sex.

Do they work?

Both are reliable so long as they are fitted and used correctly, and they can help protect against some sexually transmitted diseases.

The sheath or condom

This is the method a man can use. He pulls the sheath on to his erect penis and leaves it there until his sperm have been released. It's safer if the woman puts contraceptive cream in her vagina as well.

Does it work?

Again, it is safe if correctly used and the condom doesn't burst. More and more people are using the sheath now because it is the best available protection against infection from the AIDS virus.

The IUD (inter-uterine device) or coil

This is made of plastic or metal and has a small piece of copper wire attached to it. It is fitted inside the woman's womb by a doctor. No one is sure how it works, but it is thought to prevent a fertilized egg from attaching itself to the wall of the womb where it can begin to grow into a foetus.

Does it work?

The IUD is a reliable way of preventing pregnancy. Side-effects may be heavy or prolonged periods, or cramp-like pains. Occasionally the woman may expel it from her body.

FOR YOUR FOLDERS

1 Use the information in this section to design a leaflet on contraception for thirteen to fifteen year olds.

2 Read the case studies carefully, then put yourself in the shoes of both the mother and the father of the children. Write a piece for your favourite magazine describing your life, your thoughts and your feelings.

KEY IDEA

The older you get the more important it is that you learn about contraception. You should also learn about how girls and boys feel about sex, respect, trust and love.

Case studies

1 'When you first have your baby, your friends think this is a novelty, and for the first couple of months they are round all the time, but eventually they all drift away until you are lucky if you see them once or twice a week.

   'Contraception should be talked about more in schools and sex education improved to help prevent so many teenage pregnancies. Life as a single young mum is very difficult and can be prevented if the girl and the boy have more information on contraception.'

   (Louisa, aged eighteen)

2 'I'm missing my teenage life. When I'm eighteen I won't be able to go to the pub with my friends because I've got a baby to look after. Now that I have a baby I never have money to spend on myself. I used to think I'd be a nursery nurse but now I don't want to. I couldn't watch other folks' bairns all day and then have to come home and watch my own.'

   (Donna, aged fifteen)

3 'Being pregnant means you miss a whole chunk of your life. Overnight you have lost your childhood. It's never the same again. Even going to the park is different. I just think of all the times I went with my pals and how we mucked about and laughed.'

   (Lyanne, aged fifteen)

37 ABORTION •••••••••••••••••••••••••••••••••

Abortion is the removal from the womb of a growing **foetus** (the unborn child in the womb). The issue of abortion has created lots of discussion in the UK and across the world. It is an issue that affects thousands of people every year. It is something that these people, especially women, have to make a big decision about, one way or another.

The Law

In 1967 a law about abortion was passed in Parliament. The **Abortion Act** said that a person shall not be guilty of the unlawful ending of a pregnancy if:

- *the operation is carried out by a registered doctor and in a registered hospital (unless it is an emergency)*
- *two registered doctors agree that by carrying on with the pregnancy there would be a risk to the physical or mental health of the mother, or that there is a risk that the foetus would be born with a serious physical or mental handicap.*

In 1990 another law was passed called the **Human Fertilization and Embryology Act**. This Act says that an abortion is acceptable if:

- *the pregnancy is not longer than 24 weeks*
- *the pregnancy involves risk to the mental and physical health of the pregnant woman or any existing children of the family*
- *there is a substantial risk that if the child were born it would suffer from serious handicaps.*

For your folders

1 In what cases might two doctors perform an abortion?

2 Complete the following sentences.

- *Abortion may be carried out if the pregnancy is no longer than ...*
- *Abortion may be carried out if there is a risk to ...*

Abortion – right or wrong?

You have looked at what the law says about abortion. However, there are some people who believe that the law is wrong and abortions should not be allowed.

There are many reasons why people may believe abortion is wrong and many reasons why people may believe that under certain circumstances abortion is acceptable. The issue of abortion shows us that when people discuss issues of right and wrong, there are many ideas to think about.

In groups

In groups of about ten, read the following arguments for and against abortion. Using some of these arguments discuss what you think about abortion.

The case against abortion

- *The unborn child (called the foetus) is a separate human being. It is never just a part of a mother's body.*
- *By letting women have abortions, society is taking the easy way out. We should create a society where no child is unwanted.*
- *A foetus has a right not to be killed.*
- *People with the most serious handicaps can lead happy lives.*
- *A foetus is a potential human being. One day it could be a person.*

An Operation Rescue (an anti-abortion group) protest in New York

A Pro-choice demonstration in New York

- *Abortions can go wrong. They can leave mental and physical scars on a woman.*
- *If people were better educated to use contraceptives (see Unit 36), and single mothers were better cared for, there wouldn't be a need for abortion.*

The case for abortion

- *Every woman has a right to control her own body and make her own decision about abortion. She shouldn't be forced to make that decision by anyone else.*

- *It's not easy to know when life begins. What does life actually mean – cell, growth, heart beating, a soul?*

- *There's no such thing as 100% safe contraception.*

- *If abortions are made illegal, women will go to illegal clinics (known as **back-street abortionists**) where their lives could be at risk.*

- *Every child has a right to be a wanted child. Abortions save thousands of children from being unwanted and save society from many problems.*

- *If a woman is raped and becomes pregnant, then offering an abortion is a kind and practical way of helping her.*

- *It is a terrible experience for a fourteen year old girl to go through childbirth and then have to give the baby up for adoption because she can't possibly cope with being a mother.*

'We have been created by Almighty God in His own image and likeness. No pregnancy is unplanned because no baby can be made unless Almighty God has planned it, and has decided to bring that individual personality into the world. What has actually happened in our society is that clever arguments have convinced those who don't believe in God to think it's right to kill unborn babies. They have argued that this killing is all right and even necessary for people's happiness and the good of society.' (A Roman Catholic view)

'Humanists regard abortion as better than bringing unwanted babies into the world. It is a mistake to say that Humanists are in favour of abortion; no one can be in favour of abortion, which, except in unforeseen circumstances, is the result of failed contraception. We think there will probably always be a certain number of unplanned pregnancies and that the mothers concerned should have the complete choice of either early abortion or keeping the baby.' (A Humanist view)

'It is the woman and not the doctor who goes through the abortion operation or continues the pregnancy and has the baby. We believe that it should be for the woman to decide in the light of her own moral beliefs and personal situation. It is not for doctors nor anyone else to impose their moral or religious beliefs on others. No one can know better than the woman herself what is right for her.'

(Doctors for a Woman's Choice on Abortion)

38 AIDS

Factfile

- You cannot catch AIDS (**Acquired Immune Deficiency Syndrome**). What is caught and can be passed on (**transmitted**) is a virus called HIV, which stands for **Human Immunodeficiency Virus**.

- HIV can't be spread by sneezing or coughing, nor can it be caught by touching a carrier (somebody with the infection), or anything a carrier has touched – cutlery, crockery, food, toilet seats etc.

- The main way the virus is spread is when body fluids come into contact.

- Infection can pass from the blood, semen or vaginal fluid of one person to another person's bodily fluids.

- The virus can be passed on during sexual intercourse, or if people share injection needles.

- A mother can pass the virus onto her child while it is developing in the womb, or through breastfeeding.

- If a person tested is found to be **HIV antibody positive**, they have met the virus at some time.

- If a person is HIV antibody positive, this does not necessarily mean that they have AIDS or will develop AIDS.

- Pneumonia and cancer are illnesses sometimes found in people suffering from AIDS.

- What happens is, the body's immune system (which normally fights disease) breaks down leaving the person's body open to infection and illness.

- There is, as yet, no known cure for AIDS.

- 'Safer sex' means choosing sexual activities which cut down the risk of body fluids coming into contact.

- Using a **condom** (Johnny, sheath, rubber, Durex, Mates) helps to make intercourse safer.

- In a recent survey, carried out by the charity, Barnardos, 500 eleven to thirteen year old boys and girls were interviewed about AIDS. It was found that:

  - most children heard about AIDS from television and not from their school lessons or their parents

  - many children as young as eight or nine years old have heard about AIDS

  - many children thought that HIV or AIDS affected 'other people', for example, pop stars, alcoholics, drug addicts, and they did not fully realize that unless people are careful **everyone is at risk**.

"I was only eighteen when I first met him. He was quite a hunk...and I really fancied him. We used to go to the cinemas, maybe go in to town. My mum liked him. It was just great. I mean I couldn't have asked for nothing better. But I never thought for one minute that he could be HIV positive, because I trusted him. Things could have been very different if we'd used condoms."

SUSAN IS HETEROSEXUAL AND HIV POSITIVE.

HEALTH
EDUCATION
AUTHORITY

FOR DISCUSSION

- *What decisions should a person make about their general hygiene to avoid contact with the virus?*
- *What decisions should a person make about their sexual activity?*
- *When should children be first introduced to the issue of AIDS?*
- *If a school pupil is HIV positive, how can they be supported and helped in school?*
- *AIDS may be incurable but what can families and teachers do to make sure young people don't end up feeling frightened or helpless?*
- *How should the Government keep us informed about AIDS or HIV?*
- *After carefully reading the factfile, discuss some of the wrong ideas that people sometimes have about AIDS or HIV.*

ADVERTISEMENT SCAN

1 Look at the advertisements in this section. They are part of the campaign to help people learn about the spread of HIV and AIDS. Break up into groups of three or four and discuss:

- *who you think the advertisements are aimed at*
- *if you think the advertisements work, do they:*

  frighten you

  inform you (tell you the facts)?

2 Do you think they are the sort of advertisements that will make people change their behaviour?

3 Using some of the information in this section, design your own advertisement. Be careful to make sure your information is accurate. After you've done the advertisement, show it to a friend to check that it is accurate.

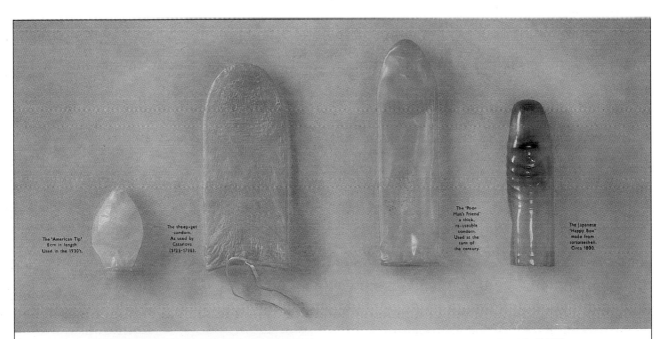

The 'American Tip'
8cm in length.
Used in the 1930's.

The sheep-gut condom.
As used by Casanova
(1725-1798).

The 'Poor Man's Friend'
a thick, re-useable condom.
Used at the turn of the century.

The Japanese 'Happy Box' made from tortoiseshell. Circa 1800.

SEX HASN'T CHANGED MUCH OVER THE YEARS. FORTUNATELY CONDOMS HAVE.

There's nothing new about having to take precautions when making love. In the past, people contracting gonorrhoea risked becoming sterile. Before penicillin was invented, syphilis could kill. Nowadays of course, we have to protect ourselves from HIV.

Fortunately, modern condoms are stronger and safer than ever before. They're also a lot more sensitive. So if the world's greatest lover made do with sheep gut, surely you can use a condom.

FOR MORE INFORMATION OR ADVICE ABOUT AIDS OR HIV, PHONE THE FREE NATIONAL AIDS HELPLINE ON 0800 567 123. IT'S OPEN 24 HOURS A DAY AND IS COMPLETELY CONFIDENTIAL.

HEALTH EDUCATION AUTHORITY

39 THE GIFT OF LIFE • • • • • • • • • • • • • • • •

Over the last few years there have been great steps made in medical science. A man and woman who are unable to have children of their own are **infertile**. Infertile people can now be helped in many ways. Here are some of the ways that that are open to them.

Artificial insemination

The male partner's semen, or the semen of an anonymous donor (someone who has given his semen), is placed into the mother artificially.

In vitro fertilization (test tube babies)

The ovum (egg) is taken from the mother and fertilized with a man's sperm in a laboratory. The embryo is then put into the mother's womb.

Egg donation

An ovum donated (given) by another woman is fertilized by sperm from the father and the embryo is put into the mother's womb.

Embryo donation

This is like egg donation, except that the ovum is fertilized by sperm from a donor. This method is used when a man and woman are both infertile.

Surrogacy

Another woman gives birth to a child for a woman who can't become pregnant, and hands the child over at birth.

Scientists also study embryos to increase their knowledge about human development. These methods raise a lot of questions about right and wrong.

The Law

Because of all the questions that these issues raise, laws have been passed to protect people. Here are some of these laws:

● *People who donate semen or eggs can remain anonymous (that is, nobody can be told their name).*

● *The number of children born to a donor should be limited to ten.*

● *The woman who gives birth as a result of an egg or embryo donation is regarded as the child's natural mother.*

● *No human embryo should be kept alive outside the womb or used for research beyond fourteen days after fertilization.*

Christian viewpoints

Here are two Christian viewpoints about medical research on embryos.

'The human embryo has the right to be treated with respect. Test-tube babies, are indeed babies, and embryos cannot be used, frozen or simply left to die without bringing into question the whole area of human rights. Human beings are not to be treated as a means to an end.'

(The Catholic Truth Society)

*'Human beings are made in the image of God. (**Genesis 1: 26**). This gives them a unique place in creation. To treat them, not as persons to be respected, but as things which may be used is to **violate** (not treat properly) this God-given nature.'*

(The Church of England)

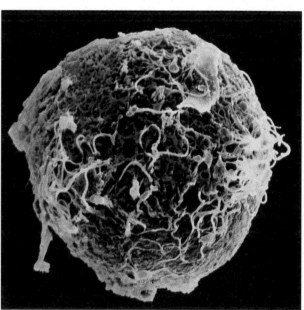

This is a photogragh of a magnified egg surrounded by sperm (the blue strands) from in vitro fertilization

MY TWIN MIRACLES

Look of love for the tiny babies with two mums

A mother cuddled her miracle twins yesterday and the woman who made their births possible was there to share her joy.

The women's amazing Mother's Day pact makes Rona Walker's family complete – five years after doctors told her she could never become a parent.

Rona was at the bedside during surrogate mother Stephanie Gates' gruelling seven-hour labour. They shared tears of delight when Alan and Fiona – a healthy 6 lb 1 oz and 5 lb 13 oz respectively eventually came into the world at Aberdeen's maternity hospital.

It was the second time that Stephanie had helped Rona fulfil her dream.

It was after losing twins and having her womb removed to save her life that Rona, now 36, was told she could never have children.

But two years later she was holding her baby daughter Kathleen – thanks to Stephanie who readily agreed to carry her baby.

Millions of TV viewers saw Stephanie weep as she handed over the tiny girl, conceived by artificial insemination from Rona's helicopter pilot husband Mark.

But the QED cameras had stopped rolling when Stephanie whispered to Rona, 'I'll help you again.' This time, Stephanie acted as host to Rona's own eggs fertilized artificially then implanted in her womb.

Stephanie was just 20 when she agreed to carry the couple's first child. 'I felt I wanted to do something useful with my life,' she said.

'When I met Rona, I felt an overwhelming urge to help her after all she had been through. It seemed natural to help her again when the time was right.'

Stephanie, who is now married with a daughter of her own, said, 'I found it quite easy to hand Kathleen over or I would never have agreed to do it again.

'She was conceived in love, but not my love. I feel exactly the same about the twins.'

Rona – not her real name to protect her family – said, 'Stephanie is amazing. I will never be able to repay her. No one can match giving the gift of life.'

(Today, 22 March 1993)

THINKING POINTS

Five parents? One would be the woman who actually carries and gives birth to the child. Two others, its genetic parents (the mother who donates the egg and the father who donates the sperm). Finally, the child's parents, the infertile couple who will take the baby home and call the child theirs.

FOR DISCUSSION

- *We should not interfere with nature.*
- *The real parents are those who bring up the child.*
- *Humans, by interfering with nature, are playing at being God.*
- *A little knowledge is a dangerous thing.*

FOR YOUR FOLDERS

1 Explain the following.
artificial insemination, test-tube babies, egg donation, embryo donation, surrogacy, fertilization.

2 Explain how it is possible for a child to have five parents.

3 What do you think might be the dangers and problems of surrogacy?

4 Explain some of the ideas mentioned in the Christian viewpoints.

TALKING POINTS

- *'I found it quite easy to hand Kathleen over ...'*
- *'No one can match giving the gift of life.'*

40 DRUGS ••••••••••••••••••••••••••••••••

Check out the facts

1 Drugs and solvents are powerful **chemicals** that can change how you think, feel and behave. Using any drug or solvent can be very dangerous.

2 People take drugs or solvents for different reasons. Some are just seeing what they are like. Others take them because they like how drugs or solvents make them feel or to help them forget about other problems they are having. *Some people find it hard to stop using drugs or solvents once they start.*

3 There are many types of drugs and solvents. The **effect** they have depends on: what sort of drug or solvent is taken; how powerful it is; how much is used; and the way it is taken. It is not easy to tell what is in a drug or how powerful it is. Drugs are often given other names when they are sold. This may mean that people take drugs without knowing exactly what is in them, which can put them at even greater risk.

4 Did you know that all **medicines** contain at least one drug? Medicines can help cure illness and some people depend on them to stay alive but, like all drugs, they can be very dangerous if not used properly. All medicines come with exact instructions about how and when they should be used. You should never use medicines that a doctor has prescribed to someone else.

5 The two most commonly used drugs are **alcohol** and **tobacco**. They are sold in shops and pubs but can cause major health problems.

6 **Cannabis** is the most widely used of the illegal drugs. Some people do not get much effect from cannabis. Others think that it makes them feel more relaxed. But, because cannabis is usually smoked with tobacco, if people smoke a lot of cannabis they can damage their lungs.

7 **Ecstasy** is really a chemical called 3,4-methylenedioxymethamphetamine which was invented 80 years ago. It comes as tablets which people swallow to make them feel as if they have more energy. The problem is that when the drug wears off after a few hours people feel tired and depressed. *Using Ecstasy may cause brain damage. Some young people have died as a result of Ecstasy use.*

8 **Solvents** are household products that give off a gas or fumes. Some types of glue, lighter fuel and many aerosol sprays contain solvents. Solvents are sniffed or sprayed into the mouth. The effects are a bit like being drunk but solvents often contain highly dangerous chemicals. *These can and do kill.*

9 Other drugs such as **amphetamine**, **heroin** and **cocaine** are also dangerous. People sometimes inject these drugs which puts them at risk of becoming infected with HIV, the virus which causes AIDS (See Unit 38).

10 Like most countries, Britain has strict laws against people, having, selling or passing on many types of drugs. Some people also steal or commit other crimes to get the money to pay for drugs. The main law against drugs is called the **Misuse of Drugs Act 1971**. The maximum penalty under this law is a life prison sentence.

11 It is *against the law* for shopkeepers to sell solvents to young people if they think they will misuse them. Shops and pubs are not allowed to sell alcohol to young people who are under eighteen years or to sell them tobacco if they are under sixteen years.

12 The best way to avoid problems with drugs and solvents is not to take them.

Solvent abuse

Some young people experiment with solvents. They become intoxicated by breathing in fumes from glues, aerosols, correction fluids, petrol, nail varnish remover and thinners. It is estimated that every week at least two young people die from solvent abuse or 'sniffing'. Children die from suffocation, choking on their own vomit and accidents when they are 'high'.

Why do people take solvents?

Some reasons might include:

- *Solvents are cheap and easy to steal or buy.*
- *Sniffing can be an alternative to alcohol.*
- *Sniffing can be seen as being exciting, because it is dangerous and is done in a group.*
- *Doing something seen as shocking by adults can seem attractive to young people.*
- *Some people sniff because their friends are trying it.*
- *Hallucinations, although often dangerous and frightening, are seen as being exciting.*
- *Hallucinations make people 'escape from the real world'. For a short while, it may stop somebody thinking about their problems, but afterwards it will make things worse.*

FOR DISCUSSION
It's OK to say 'No'

You meet up with some friends in the park who invite you to join in the glue-sniffing session. You know glue-sniffing is dangerous and want to say 'No'. What do you think is the best way to say 'No', so that you keep your friends, but make sure they won't put pressure on you again?

- *Make up an excuse and leave?*
- *Give in and join them?*
- *Make fun of them?*
- *Change the subject? ('Let's go into town.')*
- *Stall? ('I don't feel like it now – maybe later.')*
- *Tell the truth, and give your reasons? ('No thanks. I've decided not to be a sniffer.')*

Christian and Muslim teachings

'Surely you know that you are God's temple and that God's spirit dwells in you!'

(1 Corinthians 3: 16–17)

'Do not harm yourselves or others.'

(Sayings of Muhammad, the Hadith)

A group of glue-sniffers

FOR YOUR FOLDERS

1 Why do you think some young people experiment with drugs and solvents?

2 What do you think are the dangers?

3 Drugs and crime are related. Should some less harmful drugs like cannabis be legalized?

4 What do you think it means to say you are 'God's temple'?

5 Design an anti-drugs poster entitled 'It's OK to say "No"'.

41 ANIMAL MAGIC ●●●●●●●●●●●●●●●●●●●●

Animals have always been an important part of human activity. All the world religions teach that human beings should treat animals with respect. Here are just a few examples of what they teach about animals.

Views of the world religions

Bahá'í faith

'Educate the children in their infancy in such a way that they may become exceedingly kind and merciful to the animals.'

('Abdu'l-Bahá, Revelations, 303)

Christianity

'Aren't five sparrows sold for two pennies? Yet not one sparrow is forgotten by God.'

(Luke 12: 6)

Islam

'There is not a beast on the earth but God is responsible for its sustenance. He knows its lair and its resting place.'

(Qur'an 11: 8)

Judaism

'A righteous man pays attention to the needs of his animal.'

(Proverbs 12: 10)

Factfile

● *About half the families in Britain have a pet – more than seven million dogs and five million cats.*

● *At any one time it is estimated that about half a million dogs are left by their owners to roam the streets.*

● *Because many owners abandon their dogs about 1000 dogs – many quite healthy – are put down every day.*

● *Stray dogs are thought to cause problems on farms. Every year more than 10 000 farm animals are attacked.*

● *Out of every five dogs, about three have a roundworm, Toxocara canis, inside them. The eggs of these worms pass out of the dog in its excrement and lie on the ground. If children accidentally swallow them they can*

become ill and even blinded. About 50 children's eyesight is damaged each year by the disease.

● *The Dangerous Dog Act of 1991 makes it illegal to allow any dog to be dangerously out of control in a public place. The law also made it illegal to breed or sell Pit Bull terriers, Japanese Tosa, the Dogo Argentino and the Fila Braziliero. These dogs should be muzzled when in public places and they must also be in the charge of a responsible person over the age of sixteen. Rottweilers are not on the list of specially controlled dogs.*

Pets can bring us happiness, but they also bring responsibilities

Taking responsibility

Owners of pets are **responsible** for them. To be responsible means thinking and acting in such a way that the animals are cared for and they don't affect other people's happiness. In a way, having a pet teaches us responsibility because we know that if we don't care for it, it will suffer, and in some cases other people will suffer.

Case study 1

'My name is Jim. Last Sunday I went out on my bike with my mum. I was riding along when some dogs ran out and knocked me over. One of them kept biting me and wouldn't let go. It hurt. I had to go to hospital. I've got lots of stitches in my arms and legs.'

Case study 2

'My name is Trina. One Saturday my nine year old son came home after playing in the local park. He was covered in dog-dirt. I made him go and have a bath and put his clothes in the washing machine. That night he had dreadful tummy pains and was violently sick all night. The doctor later told me that my son had caught toxocariasis. I was terrified because I'd heard it had blinded a little boy in Lancashire. My son was lucky he recovered but I now believe owners who let their dogs pooh on parkland are totally irresponsible.'

Case study 3

'My name is Muhammad. One night I found a cat on my doorstep. It looked very ill. I recognized it as belonging to Mr G. our neighbour. I told Mr G. that he ought to take his cat to the vet. Two days later the cat turned up again. This time it looked even worse and when I returned it to Mr G. he swore at me and told me to mind my own business. In the morning the cat was back. My mum phoned up the RSPCA and we took the cat to a vet. The next we heard was that Mr G. had been fined. His cat was dying of cancer and he'd allowed the animal to suffer unnecessarily.'

FOR YOUR FOLDERS

1 After reading these three case studies, answer the following questions.

(a) Do you think the owners of all the pets mentioned should be punished?

(b) If so, how should they be punished?

(c) Invent ten laws that would protect animals from humans, and humans from animals.

2 Using one of the religious quotes, design a poster on caring for animals.

3 Write a short article (about 50 words) on the theme of 'Pets and Responsibility'.

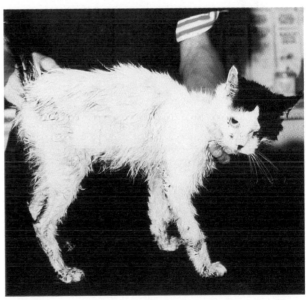

Humans sometimes treat animals very badly

Healing

In many different cultures throughout history, animals have been thought of as being special and often people have worshipped them. Early Christians believed that animals had healing powers. Today, some scientists use animals as pets to help people – for example very withdrawn children or elderly people – to feel they have something to love and look after, which helps them feel better about themselves.

42 ANIMAL RIGHTS ●●●●●●●●●●●●●●●●●●●

Do animals have rights? Over the centuries people have often treated animals in a way that suggests that they thought animals hadn't got rights. In the Bible it says, 'Be fruitful and multiply, and fill the earth and subdue it; and have dominion over the fish of the sea and over the birds of the air and over every living thing that moves upon the earth' *(Genesis: 1: 28)*.

However, to 'have dominion' does not mean that we should hunt animals for sport, imprison them in zoos, make them do stupid tricks for us in circuses, use them for medical experiments, torture them and so on. It means that we should be responsible in the way we treat animals.

Whales have been the largest-brained creatures on the planet for 30 times as long as humans have existed at all. Today their very existence is under threat because of pollution and hunting.

KEY QUESTION

Do animals have rights?
Read the following viewpoint.

'Animals feel pain – therefore they shouldn't be made to suffer unnecessarily. Animals have intelligence. This of course varies, say between whales and chickens, but nevertheless, because they all have some intelligence, they have rights.

'Animals are unique, special and sacred and, as such, every living thing on earth has a right to live. In the Genesis account of creation, the words "according to its kind" are used. This means that all living things exist on earth to grow and develop in their own special and unique way. Therefore, humans have no right to interfere with other life forms. They have a right to grow, develop, breed, give birth, care for their young, eat, play, sleep.

'Animals are an important part of our rich and beautiful planet and as such have a right to be here. Animals have emotions. They feel sadness when their young are slaughtered before their very eyes. They feel frightened by a man with a gun. They live on the same planet as us and should therefore all be treated with respect.'

(Author's interview)

THINKING POINT

'What is man without the beasts? If all the beasts were gone, man would die from a great loneliness of spirit.'

(Chief Seattle)

GROUP WORK

In three groups, discuss the following questions. Afterwards in one large group discuss the key question, 'Do animals have rights?'   ➤

Group A

When you get hurt, do you feel pain? When your friend gets hurt, do you feel your friend's pain? If your answer to the last question is that you can't feel your friend's pain, does this mean you think your friend isn't in pain?

If a person who is a stranger to you is injured, is it likely that the person is in pain? Can you feel a stranger's pain as you do your friend's pain? Can you feel a stranger's pain in the same way that you feel your own pain?

If by accident you step on your dog's foot, or your cat's tail, do they feel pain? Do you feel the pain which your pet feels when he's hurt? If you don't feel it, does it mean the animal feels no pain?

Group B

If your friend was hurt and couldn't talk, would you assume your friend was in no pain because they couldn't tell you about it? Do you think people who have done nothing wrong should be made to feel pain? Do you assume that animals feel no pain because they can't talk about it? Do you think that animals that have done nothing wrong should be made to feel pain? How do you feel about fox hunting, whaling and bullfighting? How do you feel about trapping? Should wild animals be treated more severely than domestic animals? In many ways, animals are like people. Is that a good reason for not killing them?

Group C

If you plant some lettuce in your garden and rabbits come and eat it at night, what should you do: kill the rabbits, teach the rabbits to stay away, or build a good fence? For some people in the world, there is no other way to get food than to kill animals. Is that right?

For some people in the world who have plenty of food, killing animals is a form of sport. Is this acceptable to you?

Some people say it is all right to eat animals because animals taste good. Is that a good reason? Suppose someone said that cats and dogs tasted good. Would that be a good reason to eat them? Suppose someone said that human beings tasted good. Would that be a good reason to eat them? Suppose someone said that it's all right to eat cats and dogs because there are too many of them. Would that be a good reason?

Despite international laws banning whaling, some countries still slaughter whales

PROJECT WORK

Over the next week do a project on Animal Rights. Use some of the ideas you've talked about in class discussions. Use photographs, cuttings and pictures from newspapers and magazines.

If you want more information for your project, or want to become involved in helping animals, write to:
Animal Aid, 7 Castle Street, Tonbridge, Kent, TN9 1BH
or:
Worldwide Fund for Nature, 11/13 Ockford Road, Godalming, Surrey, GU7 1QU.

Send an SAE and a small donation if you like with your requests.

Factfile

- *Ten million Africans were shipped as slaves to the Americas.*

- *From an original population of 600 000 the number of Australian Aborigines had fallen to 60 000 by the end of the 1890s.*

- *In the eighteenth century, 200 000 Maoris died in just 50 years in New Zealand (or Aotearoa as the Maoris call it).*

- *In Central and South America, numbers of indigenous peoples fell from 30 million to 5 million in just 50 years, after the arrival of the white man.*

- *By the year 2000 nearly all the rainforests (the home of many indigenous people) in India, Malaysia, Guatemala, Thailand and the Philippines will have disappeared.*

- *The Amazon forest is on fire. Its one million indigenous people are threatened.*

- *There are now sixteen alien people in South America to every Amazonian Indian.*

The First Peoples

Mines, dams, roads, colonization schemes, plantations, cattle ranches, telegraph wires, televisions, motor cars – we call these things **progress**. Yet they have destroyed and continue to destroy **Earth's First Peoples**, or the **indigenous** peoples. These are the peoples whose ancestors were the original inhabitants of the land and who lived on their original lands peacefully. With European colonization, the indigenous peoples all over the planet were killed, bullied, and their cultures were destroyed in the name of progress. They were **uprooted**.

Deforestation (cutting down forests), **desertification** (when soil is washed away, creating a desert where there was once fertile land) and **destruction** have ruined their land and their lives.

However, today, for the first time in 500 years of destruction, the indigenous peoples of the world are beginning to have their voices heard. They realize that they will never be able to return to their ancient ways of living, but they are protesting against progress which threatens their survival. They are opposed to the vandalism of the modern world which destroys Mother Earth.

TALKING POINTS

'The white man's advanced technological capacity has occurred as a result of his lack of regard for the spiritual path and for the way of all living things. The white man's desire for material possessions and power has blinded him to the pain he has caused Mother Earth by his quest for what he calls natural resources.'

(Thomas Banyaca, a Hopi Indian village leader)

'In the long hundred years since the white man came, I have seen my freedom disappear like the salmon going mysteriously out to sea. The white man's strange customs which I could not understand pressed me down until I could no longer breathe. And when I fought to protect my land and home I was called a savage.'

(Chief Dan George, Vancouver)

Neighbours speak

'These people have already made the place no good with their bulldozers. Our sacred places they have made no good. They mess up our land. They expose our sacred objects. This breaks our spirit .... Today we beg you that you truly stop.'

(Yungngora Community, Australia)

*F*OR YOUR FOLDERS

1 Using some of the ideas in the factfile, write an article called 'The Savages on Bulldozers'.

2 Design a poster on the theme of the First People's relationship with the land.

3 Survival International is a worldwide movement that works to support the First Peoples. Their survival is tied up with your survival. Do you want to live in a world in which the only way of life is ours? Or do you want to live on a planet rich in its differences? The choice is yours. If you send a postal order for £3 to Young Survival, 310 Edgware Road, London, W2 1DY, you will receive information and ideas that will be interesting, and will enable you to do something to save our planet.

4 Think about the word 'progress'. After reading the following ideas, write a paragraph on 'progress'.

  ● *Satellites can send pictures of the Cup Final across the world in seconds, yet every two seconds a child dies from hunger.*

  ● *We have only progressed in our Western world because we have robbed the First Peoples of Africa, the Americas and Australasia of their lands and ways of life.*

Photo A

Photo B

*P*HOTO SCAN

A famous American photographer, Diane Arbus (1923–71), once said,
'A photograph is a secret about a secret. The more it tells you, the less you know.'
Look at the two photographs. Write down what you think they are telling you. Discuss your findings with a friend. Now write down a caption for each photograph, and a caption that describes both of them together.

*T*ASKS

Look at the following words. List them according to whether you think they fit in with Photo A or Photo B.

Money	Mother Earth	Dignity
Stress	Reverence	Harmony
Confusion	Noise	Peace
Progress	Competition	Mystery
Frustration	Health	Illness
Materialism	Plain	Uniform
Pain	Decoration	Costume

It's an unfair world

How often do the words 'it's not fair!' flash across your mind? You can probably think of times with your family, at school or with your friends when you've felt hard done by.

It's the same for people all over the world. Have a look at this map.

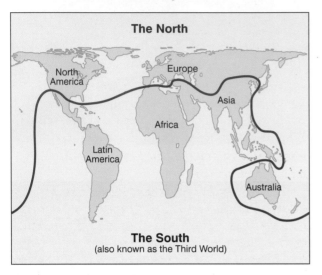

As you can see, most of the world's land surface lies in the South in Africa, Latin America and Asia.

In the North (Europe, North America and Australia), we use up **four-fifths** of the world's resources even though only **one-fifth** of the world's people live here. It's not fair on a global scale either.

Some causes of poverty

Colonialism

Hundreds of years ago, there were rich and powerful civilizations in the South. The kingdom of Great Zimbabwe, in southern Africa, was based on wealth from trading in gold and iron. The Inca kingdom stretched for thousands of miles across South America. The Incas developed advanced road systems and farming skills. Their temples can still be seen today. Between 1600 and 1900 almost every country of the South was taken over by the North. Colonialism and the slave trade allowed the colonial countries of the North to grow rich at the expense of the South.

Debt

Many countries in the South are in debt. The reasons for this go back to the 1970s when the rich countries of the North had a lot of money to spare. They lent it to poorer countries. This was fine until interest rates rose and the cost of borrowing became higher. To pay off their debts, poorer countries needed to earn more money by selling raw materials. When the prices of materials fell debts grew. Richer countries are part of the debt problem, rather than the solution. When governments are affected by problems, it is poorer people who suffer.

Unfair trade

Out of every £1 jar of coffee sold in the UK, the producing country gets 37p. Some of this money goes to the government and some to the grower. Most of the money stays in the UK, which controls the transporting, processing and distribution of coffee.

Christian Aid

There are many organizations working to make the world a better place. Two such organizations are Christian Aid and Islamic Relief. This is part of Christian Aid's statement explaining their work.

'The most effective and respectful way of improving the quality of life of the poor and powerless is to get or put back into their own hands the means to help themselves. We must help people to rebuild their own communities by providing them with schools, health care, clean water and work.

*'Christian Aid is Christian because Christian faith provides the **reason** for caring. Christians believe that God loves the world and all that is in it. They believe that God became a human in Jesus and that in a real sense they can meet God in every human being.*

*'Christian faith provides the **example** of Jesus and how He mixed with and respected those who were poor or despised by others.*

*'Christian faith provides **teaching**. Since New Testament times, true Christians have*

been committed to living out Jesus' teaching on how people should regard and treat the poor.

'Christian faith provides a *vision* of the kingdom of God. This shows what the world could be like. In a practical sense Christian Aid is Christian because it was set up by the churches of the UK and Ireland to put into action the concern of Christians for those in need. This concern is for all, whatever their race or faith.'   (Christian Aid statement)

Every year she earns enough to feed her family for 6 months.

Every morning work starts at 6am.

Every family member over 12 is working.

Every 11 hour day earns £1. Between them.

Everyone knows they deserve better.

Every donation helps them achieve it.

Every year we work to strengthen the poor in over 70 countries. Believe us, we can't do it without your help.
Name _____   Address _____

Postcode _____   To: Christian Aid, PO Box 100, London SE1 7RT. **Christian Aid**
I enclose a cheque/PO for: £10☐ £25☐ £50☐ £100☐ £200☐ Other £____   We believe in life before death

Christian Aid Week. May 17-22. Give now. Ring 0839 200 100.

Registered Charity No. 258003. Calls charged at 39p per minute cheap rate and 49p at all other times.

Islamic Relief

'Helping others is a very important part of being a Muslim. In fact, after worshipping God, it is probably the most important thing about living a good Islamic life.

'Our prophet Muhammad, peace be upon him, once said, "You are not truly a believer if you sleep with a full stomach and your neighbour is hungry."

'What is more, he did not say that the neighbour has to be of the same religion. As Muslims, we wish to help all people, whether they are Jews, Christians or of any other religion or race.

'This help should also be extended to animals. There is a famous story of how a woman, who was well known for not behaving properly, went to heaven because she gave a thirsty dog in the desert water to drink from a well.

'Of course, the reasons why we want to help people and animals are also very important. Some people like to give charity to show everyone else that they are rich, or just to give the impression that they are kind and generous.

'Muslims like to give charity in order to please Allah (God). They need to be very careful not to show off when they give charity to help people. They also have to be very careful not to expect any reward for their good action in this life.

'The reward a Muslim expects is from Allah (God) on the Day of Judgement, when acts of charity are counted among the good actions that get you into heaven.

'Those of us who work in Islamic Relief try to live up to these principles. We try our best to get help to anyone who is hungry, or homeless, or an orphan without parents, without asking for anything in return.

'Of course, sometimes we can reach only a small proportion of those in trouble, but the important thing is to try … and try your best.

'On the Day of Judgement, Allah will not be concerned with whether we were successful or not, but whether we tried our best – to please Him by helping others in trouble.'

(Islamic Relief statement)

FOR YOUR FOLDERS

Read the Christian Aid and Islamic Relief statements. Now answer the following questions for each organization.

- *Why do they feel they need to help?*
- *Why do they believe it is important to give?*
- *What did their religious leaders think about helping others?*

A Christian view of justice

Christians believe that God created everything good. God's work can be seen in every human being who has been made in the image and likeness of God.

To Christians, like members of the other great world faiths, human beings are all members of one single human family. This family is interconnected – if one member of the family suffers, then the whole family suffers. If we sit back and let others suffer, then we suffer too.

Christians believe that God wants justice in His world. However, He has given us freedom to choose between right and wrong. It is up to each individual person to work for justice in the world. Christians believe God loved the world so much that He sent us Jesus who, by His life, gave us an example of how we should live. Many Christians belong to an organization called Amnesty International. Amnesty International is not a Christian organization, but many Christians agree with its aims.

Amnesty International

Amnesty International is a worldwide movement made up of individuals who work for the release of **Prisoners of Conscience**. These are men, women and children who have been thrown into prison because of what they believe, or because of their colour, their sex, their ethnic origin or their religion.

Amnesty International works to abolish torture and the death penalty. It is a terrible thing to realize that torture is practised by over half of the governments of the world. Throughout the world thousands of people are in prison, just because of what they believe. Many may not even be given a trial. In many countries men, women and children have 'disappeared', murdered by their government, never to be seen again.

Members of Amnesty form local groups and write letters to the governments of the countries where people are being so badly treated. These letters show them that the world is watching as they torture and mistreat people. In this extract, Terry Waite, who was held hostage in Lebanon for four years, explains the importance of letter writing.

Viewpoint 1

'I'll tell you a small story which I told in Damascus. I was kept in total and complete isolation for four years. I saw no one and spoke to no one apart from a cursory word with my guards when they brought me food. And one day out of the blue a guard came with a postcard. It was a postcard showing a stained glass window from Bedford, showing John Bunyan in jail. And I looked at that card and I thought, "My word, Bunyan, you're a lucky fellow. You've got a window out of which you can look and see the sky, and here I am in a dark room. You've got a pen and ink, you can write; but here I am, I've got nothing and you've got your own clothes and a table and a chair." And I turned the card over and there was a message from someone whom I didn't know, simply saying, "We remember, we shall not forget. We shall continue to pray for you and to work for all people who are detained around the world." That thought sent me back to the marvellous work of agencies like Amnesty International and their letter writing campaigns and I would say, never despise those simple actions. Something, somewhere will get through to the people you are concerned about as it got through to me and to my fellows eventually.'

(Terry Waite, excerpts from the homecoming speech, November 1991

*T*HINGS TO DO

There are about 280 young Amnesty groups in Britain. Your class could form a group, and you can help to make the world a better place. Over the next week try to save £1 each – you might only have to go without a few sweets. Collect the class's money and send it to Young Amnesty, 99–119 Rosebery Avenue, London EC1R 4RE.

➤

Ask Amnesty to send you details of their work, and ideas for your new group. If you are wondering why you should bother, read Viewpoint 2, written by a thirteen year old boy from Chile.

'The candle burns not for us, but for all those whom we failed to rescue from prison, who were shot on the way to prison, who were tortured, who were kidnapped, who "disappeared". That's what the candle is for ...'

(Peter Benenson, founder, Amnesty International)

Viewpoint 2

'I was woken by the sound of screaming. I'd been thrown into this tiny room for three days now. Every night there was screaming. People were being tortured. My brother had died in my room before my very eyes. He'd been beaten so badly. They left his body in with me. Then, one night they came for me. Two guards dragged me by the hair into this room – it was very light. The guards were drunk. They tied me onto a bed and put electric wires on my body. I was so scared ... and then the agony began. When they'd finished with me I couldn't walk. I was in prison for three months. I never did anything wrong. Torture is the most evil thing. It has destroyed my life. Only you can help us. Please, in the name of God, help.'

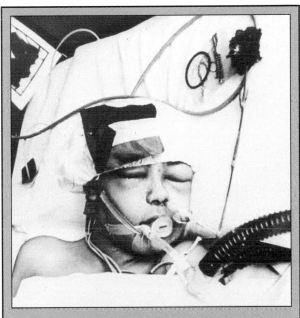

The penalty for throwing stones

Israeli-Occupied Territories

Rana al-Masri, aged thirteen, was shot in the head in 1989 by Israeli soldiers using rubber-coated metal pellets.

Palestinian children in the Occupied Territories have been victims of human rights violations by Israeli forces since the intifada (uprising) began in December 1987. Children have been shot, tortured or imprisoned after trials which may have been unfair.

Many of these children had been throwing stones at soldiers or policemen.

FOR YOUR FOLDERS

1 Why, according to Terry Waite, should we never despise the simple actions of writing a letter?

2 Why is torture 'the most evil thing', according to the thirteen year old boy from Chile?

Prisoner of conscience

Jack Mapanje, the world famous poet, spent four years in prison in Malawi. His 'crime' was that the government did not like his poetry. Jack was not even tried by a court for four years. Amnesty International, who adopted him as a Prisoner of Conscience, worked for his release and in 1991 he was finally given his freedom.

In this book you have been encouraged to think about and discuss many different issues. If you have been able to understand some of these issues a little better and have seen how others feel about them, then this book will have been a success.

Basically these issues can be divided up into three areas:

- *issues that affect individuals – personal issues*
- *issues that affect groups or communities – social issues*
- *issues that affect the world – global issues.*

These three divisions are, however, all connected. What affects a group will affect the individual and what affects an individual will affect the world.

A global village

In one sense the world today is a much smaller place than it used to be. It has been called a **global village**. This means that, like in a village, everyone knows each other and how things are going for them. We can make a telephone call to China in minutes. We can receive live pictures from anywhere in the world on our television screens. We can send messages to the other side of the world in a matter of seconds. We know what is going on all over the world.

What happens in another part of the world can affect us in our own community. This is especially true of the environment. For example, in 1986, dangerous radioactive rain fell on Britain following the explosion of a nuclear reactor in Chernobyl, in Russia.

Although the people of the world live in different nations, they are all part of one world. When spacecraft take pictures of our planet, they do not just see Britain, Africa or Australia; they see **one planet** in an enormous universe. Indeed we can call ourselves **citizens of the world**.

KEY QUESTION 1

In this book we have looked at the idea of responsibilities. As citizens of the world, what responsibilities to others do you think we have?

Careless caretakers

We have also been called **stewards** or **caretakers** of our planet. This means that the earth does not belong to us, but that we belong to the earth. Compared to the age of the earth, our individual lives are very short. During our short stay here, we have a responsibility to look after the earth, and if we are able, to leave the earth a better place for the next generation.

Sadly this has not been the case over the last hundred years or so, during which we have treated the earth very badly. Our rivers and seas, our atmosphere, our fields and forests have all suffered terribly from pollution and destruction. We have destroyed many different species of animals and birds and taken many others to the brink of extinction. What we are only recently beginning to understand is that **all things are connected**. By destroying the earth and its plants and animals, we are also destroying ourselves. We have been careless caretakers.

'There is no quiet place in the white man's cities. No place to hear the unfurling of leaves in spring or the rustle of insects' wings. The clatter only seems to insult the ears. The white man does not seem to notice the air he breathes. Like a man dying for many days, he is numb to the stench. Continue to contaminate your bed, and you will one night suffocate in your own waste.'

(Chief Seattle, 1855)

KEY QUESTION 2

How can I personally try and make the world a better place?

Greenpeace activists blocking a chemical outflow pipe

We are the lucky ones. Most of us do not know what it's like to be hungry for months or years on end. Most of us do not know what it's like to have our homes destroyed in war or see our loved ones murdered before our very eyes. Most of us do not know what it's like to have our freedom taken away, or to be maimed and tortured. But for millions of people, many of them young people like you, these things are happening at this very moment. These people are no different from you, your families or your friends. The only difference is that you are one of the lucky ones. You therefore, have the power and the ability to help them.

*I*N GROUPS

In groups of three or four discuss some of the problems that face your fellow global citizens. Make a list of some of the things in the world you feel need changing.

Working for change

There are many people working today to make the world a better place. They are working to bring peace and justice (fairness) into a world full of war, famine and injustice. During the latter part of this book you were introduced to some of these people working for the United Nations (p.44), Amnesty International (p.92); Christian Aid (p.90); Islamic Relief (p.91); Survival International (p.89), the Worldwide Fund for Nature (p.87) and Animal Aid (p.87).

Here are a few other organizations that are working to improve the world:

- *Campaign Against the Arms Trade, 11 Goodwin Street, London, N4 3HQ (working to stop businesspeople and governments selling guns and bombs)*
- *Friends of the Earth, 26–28 Underwood Street, London, N1 7IQ (working to save the planet)*
- *Greenpeace, Canonbury Villas, London, N1 2PN (working to stop the destruction of our planet)*
- *OXFAM, 274 Banbury Road, Oxford, OX2 7DZ (working to help the poorest peoples of the planet).*

*T*HINGS TO DO

All these organizations rely on donations. If everyone in your class gave just 30 pence each over the next week, you could send off a postal order for about £9 to one of these organizations. In return, the organization would send you an information pack and loads of ideas about how you could begin to make the world a better place. You have the power to help. For your own sake, your fellow global citizens' sake and for the children of the future, get organized today!

*T*HINKING POINT

'Everyone can be great. Because everybody can serve!'

(Dr Martin Luther King)

INDEX ●●●●●●●●●●●●●●●●●●●●●●●●●●●●●●●●●